T0213601

SpringerBriefs in Computer Science

More information about this series at http://www.springer.com/series/10028

Shlomo Dubnov · Kevin Burns
Yasushi Kiyoki

Cross-Cultural Multimedia Computing

Semantic and Aesthetic Modeling

 Springer

Shlomo Dubnov
University of California in San Diego
La Jolla, CA
USA

Yasushi Kiyoki
Keio University
Minato, Tokyo
Japan

Kevin Burns
The MITRE Corporation
Bedford, MA
USA

ISSN 2191-5768   ISSN 2191-5776   (electronic)
SpringerBriefs in Computer Science
ISBN 978-3-319-42871-0   ISBN 978-3-319-42873-4   (eBook)
DOI 10.1007/978-3-319-42873-4

Library of Congress Control Number: 2016946332

Printed on acid-free paper

This Springer imprint is published by Springer Nature
The registered company is Springer International Publishing AG Switzerland

Contents

About the Authors

Shlomo Dubnov is a Professor of Music and Computer Science in UCSD. He holds Ph.D. in Computer Science from Hebrew University, MSc in EE from Israel Institute of Technology (Technion) and B.Mus in Music Composition from Rubin Academy in Jerusalem. He served as a researcher at Institute for Research and Coordination in Acoustics and Music (IRCAM) in Centre Pompidou, Paris and was a visiting professor in KEIO University, Japan, and Computer Science Laboratory (LaBRI) in University of Bordeaux, France. His work on computational modeling of style and computer audition has led to development of several computer music programs for improvisation and machine understanding of music. He currently directs the Center for Research in Entertainment and Learning (CREL) at UCSD's Qualcomm Institute (Calit2) and serves as a lead editor in ACM Computers in Entertainment Journal.

Kevin Burns is a Cognitive Scientist researching human perceptions, decisions, emotions, and interactions between humans and machines—with applications to national security, industrial safety, organizational efficiency, and personal artistry. The objective across these diverse domains is to measure and model how people think and feel, as a basis for building machines that can help humans manage risk and enjoy life. Kevin is employed by The MITRE Corporation and holds engineering degrees from the Massachusetts Institute of Technology.

Yasushi Kiyoki received his B.E., M.E., and Ph.D. degrees in Electrical Engineering from Keio University in 1978, 1980 and 1983, respectively. From 1984 to 1996, he was with Institute of Information Sciences and Electronics, Univ. of Tsukuba, as Assistant Professor and then Associate Professor. In 1990 and 1991, he was in University of California at Irvine, as a visiting researcher. Since 1996, he has been with Department of Environment and Information Studies at Keio University, and from 1998 he is currently Professor. Since 2011, he is a chair and coordinator of "Global Environmental System Leader Program (GESL)" in KEIO University. His research addresses semantic computing, environmental engineering, multimedia database systems and knowledge base systems. His original semantic model is "Mathematical Model of Meaning (MMM)," and he has more than 100 paper publications related to MMM. He serves as the editor-in-chief on Information Modelling and Knowledge Bases (IOS Press). He has also served as the program chair for several international conferences, such as International Conferences on Information Modelling and Knowledge Bases (2004—Present). He was a keynote speaker in 7th IEEE International Conference on Semantic Computing, September 2013, as the title of "A Kansei: Multimedia Computing System for Environmental Analysis and Cross-Cultural Communication."

Short Description of the Book

The ability to communicate cultural codes in multimedia depends on their meaning and beauty, as perceived by different audiences around the globe. In this book we describe ongoing research on computational modeling of visual, musical, and textual contents in terms of identifying and mapping their semantic and aesthetic representations across different cultures. The underlying psychology of sense-making is quantified through analysis of aesthetics in terms of organizational and structural aspects of the contents that influence an audience's formation of expectations for future signals, violations of these expectations, and explanations of their meaning. Complexity-accuracy trade-offs in sound representation are further used to develop new computational methods that capture poietic and aesthetic aspects in music communication. Experimental studies are reported that try to characterize preferences for complexity in abstract, classical, and traditional art and music across samples of Western and Far Eastern cultures. These experiments illustrate how aesthetics can be computed in terms of semantic and information measures, highlighting commonalities and uncovering differences in aesthetic preferences across cultures and individuals.

Introduction

Art is the imposing of a pattern on experience, and our aesthetic enjoyment is recognition of the pattern.

—Alfred North Whitehead

This book represents a collective effort to define the role of computing in cultural context, allowing closer understanding of differences and similarities in aesthetic expressions and sensibilities between different cultures, as detected by the machine. This goal cannot rely purely on exploitation of existing computational tools. Cross-cultural multimedia computing is a field of research where problems of meaning or semantics are applied to cultural data, such as images, music, video, and text, with comparative analysis performed between different cultures. Reporting state-of-the-art research in this domain spans various disciplines, including but not limited to areas such as semantic computing, psychology, information theory, computer music, semiotics, and more. The development of such cultural computational tools has practical implications: culture-specific impression-based metadata can be extracted and mapped to similar impressions from another culture, associations between sounds and images can be used to create automatic media decoration models dependent on their cultural context, and many more. But most importantly, such research sheds new light on our understanding of the human aesthetic faculty, a concept referring to human ability to perceive elegance or beauty, and possibly even wit and humor, encompassed to some extent by Western term of Aesthetics and the Japanese term "Kansei" that links psychological sensibilities and emotions to aspects of product design. The Kansei approach, described in the first chapter, assumes that an artistic artifact can be described in a certain vector space, which is defined by semantic expressions (words) that represent impressions and imaginations evoked by the object in the viewer or listener. Extending the vector space approach to include aspects of expectation and surprise requires tracking of changes in the qualities of the artistic object over time. In the second chapter of this book a novel EVE' (Expectation, Violation, Explanation) model is applied to textual and visual expression, emphasizing the sequential nature of human thought process and artistic decision-making. Moreover, it is argued that generic object properties, such as complexity and order, can be used to characterize an aesthetic effect, though in ways that are different from those proposed early on in the field of computational aesthetics. This chapter also suggests and shows experimental evidence for existence of universals in perception of aesthetic properties across cultures.

Using tools and terminology of communication and information theory, the properties of the object or artistic artifact, and properties of the receiver, the viewer, or listener, are inevitably linked to each other. Such relation seems to suggest that aesthetic appreciation can be communicated based on commonalities in cognitive processing of abstract structures shared by humans across cultures. It is important to realize that these commonalities do not preclude the development of different forms of cultural expression, or development of personal preferences towards certain types of artistic expression through process of learning or enculturation. The question of relations between units and levels of structure, and their relation to aesthetic appreciation is brought up in the third chapter in the context of analysis of sound examples from Western and Far Eastern musical cultures. Borrowing from semiotic analysis of text, the question of "poietic" or compositional aspects of a work of art that are employed in its creation versus the ability to perceive its "aesthetics" is dealt through musical information dynamics analysis. It is shown that paying notice to different levels of sound detail results in very different structures and cultural paradigms between Western and Far Eastern music. The results seems to support an intuitive notion that expressive intonation and more nuanced aspects of instrumental sound production are of significance in Far Eastern traditions, while schematic and pronounced structural elements are more dominant in Western classical music. The theories, applications, and experimental results presented in this book suggest that communication across cultures is amenable to computational analysis, though our formal understanding of the cultural phenomena is only in its beginnings.

Chapter 1
A 'Kansei' Multimedia and Semantic Computing System for Cross-Cultural Communication

Abstract In the design of multimedia computing systems, one of the most important issues is how to search and analyze media data (images, music, movies and documents), according to user's impressions and contexts. This paper presents *"Kansei*-Multimedia Computing System" for realizing international and cross-cultural research environments, as a new platform of multimedia computing system. We introduce a *"Kansei"* and semantic associative search method based on the "Mathematical Model of Meaning (MMM)". The concept of *"Kansei"* includes several meanings on sensitive recognition, such as "emotion", "impression", "human senses", "feelings", "sensitivity", "psychological reaction" and "physiological reaction". MMM realizes *"Kansei"* processing and semantic associative search for media data, according to user's impressions and contexts. This model is applied to compute semantic correlations between keywords, images, music, movies and documents dynamically in a context-dependent way. This system based on MMM realizes (1) *"Kansei"* image and music search and analysis for cooperative creation and manipulation of multimedia objects and (2) Cross-cultural communications with music and images databases.

1.1 Introduction

The rapid progress of multimedia technology has realized the large scale of media data transfer and resource-accumulation in the world. Cross-cultural computing becomes an important issue in global societies and communities connected in the world-wide scope. The innovative integration of large scale multimedia data management and cross-cultural computing will lead to new cross-cultural environments in our society.

We have designed *"Kansei*-Multimedia Computing System" for realizing automatic media decoration with dynamic sub-media data selection for representing main-media as decorative multimedia. The aim of this method is to create "automatic decorative-media art" with "semantic associative computing" [1].

© The Author(s) 2016
S. Dubnov et al., *Cross-Cultural Multimedia Computing*,
SpringerBriefs in Computer Science, DOI 10.1007/978-3-319-42873-4_1

The field of "Kansei" information was originally introduced as the word "aesthetics" by Baumgrarten in 1750. The aesthetics of Baumgrarten had been established and succeeded by Kant with his ideological aesthetics [2, 3]. In the research field of multimedia database systems, it is becoming important to deal with "Kansei" information for defining and extracting media data according to impressions and senses of individual users.

1.2 The Mathematical Model of Meaning (MMM)

In this section, the outline of our semantic associative search method based on the *Mathematical Model of Meaning (MMM)* is briefly reviewed. This model has been presented in [4, 5] in detail.

The overview of the MMM is expressed as follows:

(1) A set of m words is given, and each word is characterized by n features. That is, an m by n matrix is given as the data matrix.
(2) The correlation matrix with respect to the n features is constructed. Then, the eigenvalue decomposition of the correlation matrix is computed and the eigenvectors are normalized. The orthogonal semantic space is created as the span of the eigenvectors which correspond to nonzero eigenvalues.
(3) Images and context words are characterized by using the specific features (words) and representing them as vectors.
(4) The images and context words are mapped into the orthogonal semantic space by computing the Fourier expansion for the vectors.
(5) A set of all the projections from the orthogonal semantic space to the invariant subspaces (eigen spaces) is defined. Each subspace represents a phase of meaning, and it corresponds to a context or situation.
(6) A subspace of the orthogonal semantic space is selected according to the user's impression or the image's contents, which are given as a context represented by a sequence of words.
(7) The most correlated image to the given context is extracted in the selected subspace by selecting and applying one of the metrics defined in the semantic space.

The advantages and original points of the MMM are as follows:

(1) The semantic associative search based on semantic computation for words is realized by a mathematical approach. This media search method surpasses the search methods which use pattern matching for associative search. Users can use their own words for representing impression and data contents for media retrieval, and do not need to know how the metadata of media data of retrieval candidates are characterized in databases.

(2) Dynamic context recognition is realized using a mathematical foundation. The context recognition can be used for obtaining multimedia information by giving the user's impression and the contents of the information as a context. A semantic space is created as a space for representing various contexts which correspond to its subspaces. A context is recognized by the computation for selecting a subspace.

Several information retrieval methods, which use the orthogonal space created by mathematical procedures like SVD (Singular Value Decomposition), have been proposed. The MMM is essentially different from those methods using the SVD method. The essential difference is that our model provides the important function for semantic projections which realizes the dynamic recognition of the context. That is, the context-dependent interpretation is dynamically performed by computing the distance between different media data, information resources and words. The context-dependency is realized by dynamically selecting a subspace from the entire orthogonal semantic space, according to a context. In MMM, the number of phases of contexts is almost infinite (currently 2^{2000} in the general English word space and 2^{130} in the color-image space, approximately). For semantic associative computations of "*Kansei*" information in MMM, we have constructed several actual semantic spaces, such as the general English-word space in 2000 dimensions approximately, the color-image space in 130 dimensions, and music space in 8 dimensions in the current implementations.

1.3 Cross-Cultural Computing System for Music

This section introduces a cross-cultural computing system for music, which is realized by applying MMM to "cultural-music resources." We have designed this system to promote cross-cultural understanding and communication by using cultural music. The system consists of music analysis, search and visualization functions: (1) a culture-dependent semantic metadata extraction function, which extracts both musical elements (e.g., key, pitch, tempo) and impression metadata (e.g., sad, happy, dreamy) corresponding to properties of each musical-culture, (2) a cross-cultural computing function to represent differences and similarities among various music-cultures, and (3) an easy-to-use interface function designed for helping users to join the music database creation process. The significant feature of our cross-cultural computing system is its multimedia database technology applying of "*Kansei*" impressions, to compute the cultural differences. This system extracts features of music-cultures and expresses cultural-dependent impressions by interpreting cultural-music pieces in the semantic music-space, and makes it possible to compare cultural difference and similarity in terms of impressions among various cultural music resources.

The important objective of this system is to evoke impressions and imaginations including the cultural diversity by representing various impression-based responses to music resources from different cultures. There are two main scenarios designed to allow users to attain impressions and imaginations: (1) how a music piece would be interpreted among different music-cultures and (2) how an impression would be composed in different music-cultures. The system realizes metadata extraction, search, visualization, and search functions which have been designed in a culture-oriented way. Two music-domains, impressions (e.g., sad, dreamy and happy) and musical elements (e.g., key, pitch and tempo) are utilized to compare cultural-differences. In this system implementation, it is important how to deal with semantic heterogeneity when impressions are variously expressed among different music-cultures. This system provides a culture-dependent impression metadata extraction method to tackle this challenge with participation of users. Here, "culture" is defined as the collective knowledge which distinguishes the members of one culture group (human group) from another group's [6].

In addition, we consider "cross-cultural computing" as the similarity and difference computation in each domain belonged to common cultural determinants among several cultures. We also define the term "impression" as the culture-dependent emotion-based response which people of a culture react to any music piece (e.g., sad, dreamy and happy).

In the system implementation, we use traditional music as common cultural determinant. Firstly, music is a powerful medium to express human emotion [7], and some data show that many people are using traditional music as the main means to discover a new culture [8]. In addition, Brown in [9] also asserts that music likely has been a main contributor to reinforcing "groupishness" by offering the opportunities to formalize and maintain group identity. That is, music in a given culture, called music-culture, can become a vital part to formalize the "culture identity".

1.3.1 System Architecture

The cross-cultural computing system for music consists of eight main functions, as shown in Fig. 1.1, and we have shown the system architecture in detail in [10]. Those functions are grouped into five layers including multimedia databases, metadata generation, search, visualization, and user interface. The overview of each function is described as follows:

(F-1) Musical Element Analyzer extracts music metadata of six basic musical elements (key, tempo, pitch, rhythm, harmony and melody) from music MIDI files.

(F-2) Culture-dependent Impression Metadata Extractor extracts weighted impression words (e.g. sad, happy) of a music piece as metadata from culture-dependent musical elements-impression E-I matrices, created by (F-3) and (F-4), and the elements' values computed in (F-1).

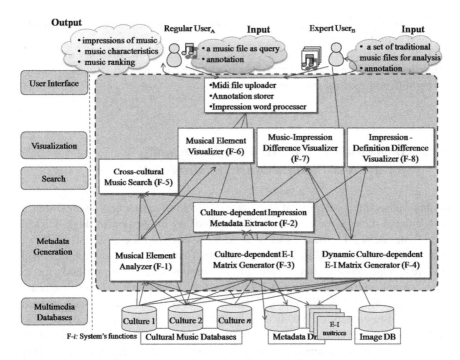

Fig. 1.1 System architecture of our culture-oriented music analysis system

(F-3) Culture-dependent E-I Matrix Generator is a matrix creation function. This function creates a specific matrix representing the relationship between musical elements and impressions of a particular musical-culture by using music samples and filtering functions.

(F-4) Dynamic Culture-dependent E-I Matrix Generator is an extending part of (F-3). This function is to automatically provide a prototype of an E-I matrix from a set of culture-based music files and provide an easy-to-use interface allowing users to amend this matrix.

(F-5) Cross-cultural Music Search calculates the correlations between impression, expressed as a context-query given by keywords or music, and impressions of music pieces in cultural music databases by applying MMM as the impression-based semantic associative computing system with a cross-cultural music space. And then, this function provides music ranking as a music-search result, according to correlations between the context query and the impressions of music pieces.

(F-6) Musical Elements Visualizer provides the visualization of musical elements of any music piece which is uploaded by users.

(F-7) Music-impression Difference Visualizer displays various impressions of music pieces; these impressions are analyzed from the viewpoints of different musical-cultures. Image data are also integrated to support users in understanding the diverse impressions.

(F-8) Impression-definition Difference Visualizer shows the diversity of musical properties (musical elements) to express a particular impression (e.g. sad, happy) among different musical-cultures.

1.3.2 Impression-Based Metadata Extraction for a Cross-Cultural Music Environment

In this subsection, we present a semantic metadata extraction method for a cross-cultural music environment, the key technology in our system (Figs. 1.2 and 1.3). Basic ideas for extracting cultural features in music are as follows: (1) we consider Western classical music as a part of cross-cultural music environment, and (2) we create our culture-dependent impression extraction method for a cross-cultural music environment by extending an automatic music metadata extraction method for Western classical music. We apply the music-analysis method [11] to embark on our method for extracting cultural music features. This method shown in Fig. 1.2 extracts six musical elements of each music piece (key, tempo, pitch, rhythm, harmony, melody) then converts them to impression words (e.g. sad, happy) by using a lexico-media transformation matrix T based on the music psychological research of Hevner [12].

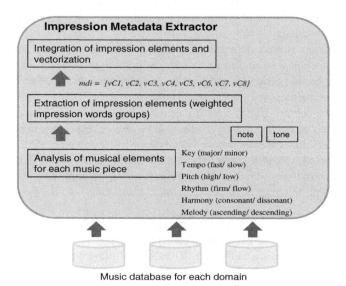

Fig. 1.2 The impression metadata extraction method in music

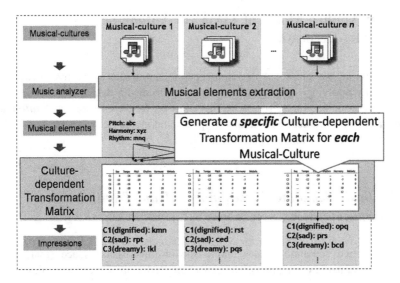

Fig. 1.3 The cross-cultural music environment for extracting cultural-dependent impressions from cultural-music resources

Hevner has proposed eight categories of adjectives to represent music impressions (dignified, sad, dreamy, serene, graceful, happy, exciting, and vigorous) and she also devised a correlation table between these adjective groups and six musical elements. However, Hevner's table is suitable to only Western classical music. For creating a cross-cultural environment, as shown in Fig. 1.3, we have designed a culture-dependent metadata extraction as follows: (1) we adopt the schema of Hevner's table and set it as a unified schema to create a table expressing musical elements-impressions relationship in database and (2) we create our process to express specific musical elements–impressions in the E-I transformation matrix T for each musical-culture by using music samples and filtering functions. Hereinafter, we call this matrix T as E-I matrix T.

Our cross-cultural computing system for music is a novel platform to evoke users' imaginations and impressions for the cultural diversity by presenting the variety of emotional responses to music from different cultures. This system makes it possible to realize universal impression analysis to various music-cultures sharing various music-properties.

We have applied this method to several multimedia database applications, such as image and music database search by impressionistic classification. We have introduced these research results in [1, 4, 5]. Through these studies, we have created a new meta-level knowledge base environment by applying those methods to data retrieval, data integration and data mining [13].

1.4   An Applied Model of MMM to Automatic Media-Decoration

In this section, we present a new concept of "automatic decorative-multimedia creation" by applying the MMM to automatic sub-media data selection for decorating a main-media object. To realize this concept, we have defined an "*automatic media decoration model*" with semantic spaces and media-decoration functions [1]. The overview of this model is shown in Fig. 1.4.

1.4.1   Basic Semantic Spaces and a Media-Transmission Space

We define two semantic spaces and a media-transmission space (matrix) for computing semantic correlations between main-media objects and sub-media.

(1) M-Space (Main-media semantic space):

Each main-media object or each impression word expressing impression of a main-media object is defined as an M-Space vector with m main-media-features.

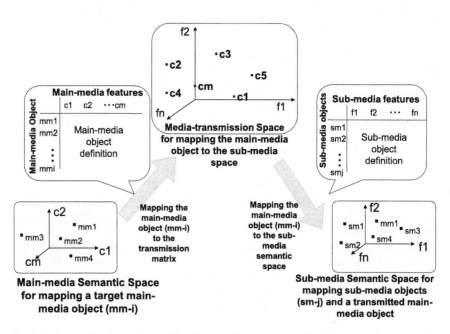

Fig. 1.4 Automatic decorative-multimedia creation system with the semantic associative computation method

(2) S-Space (Sub-media semantic space):

Each sub-media object or each impression word expressing impressions in a sub-media object is defined as an S-Space vector with n sub-media-features. In this space, various sub-media objects are mapped in advance, as retrieval candidates, in S-Space for decorating the main-media object.

(3) MS-Space (Main-media and Sub-media transmission space):

Each of m features of Main-media is expressed in the n features of Sub-media in the MS space. The MS-space is defined as a (m, n) matrix for transmitting an M-space vector into its corresponding S-space vector.

1.4.2 Basic Functions for Media Decoration

In this method, basic functions for decoration of a main-media object with sub-media are defined:,

Step-1   maps a target main-media object onto the M-Space as the M-space vector for the decoration target, by expressing the object as an m-dimensional vector with the m features.

Step-2   computes correlation values between the M-space vector and each sub-media feature in the MS-Space (Main-media and Sub-media transmission space) by the Mathematical Model of Meaning (MMM), and creates an S-Space vector (target-S-Space vector) as the transmitted vector of the main-media object.

Step-3   maps the target S-Space vector expressing the main-media object onto the S-Space.

Step-4   executes the semantic associative search processes by the MMM between the target S-Space vector and the candidate sub-media objects which have been mapped onto the S-Space in advance. (In MMM, the target S-Space vector is mapped as a context vector in S-Space, and candidate sub-media objects are mapped as retrieval candidates in S-Space.)

Step-5   outputs semantic ranking of sub-media objects as the result of our semantic associative search processes, and selects one of the sub-media objects with high correlation values to the target main-media object.

Step-6   renders the target main-media object with the selected sub-media object for decorating the main-media presentation with the selected sub-media data.

1.5 Media Design with "Automatic Decorative Multimedia Creation"

In this section, we present several applications of the automatic decorative-multimedia creation by our semantic associative computation method.

1.5.1   Music Decoration with Images

This application is automatic "music decoration with images," as shown in Figs. 1.5 and 1.6. This decoration process consists of 6 steps.

Step-1   generates the metadata (in a form of a vector in the "music semantic space") of music-media object, as a main-media object.

Our research project has proposed several automatic impression metadata generation methods for music [10, 11, 14, 15]. In this step, we use the metadata generation method to create impression metadata of music data [11, 14]. This method applies the music psychology by Hevner [12] to automatic extraction of music impression.

Step-2   generates the metadata (in a form of a vector in the "image semantic space") of each image-media object in the image collection, as the collection of sub-media object. Our research project has also proposed several impression metadata generation methods for images. In this step, we apply one of the metadata generation methods to create metadata of image data [4, 5, 16–18].

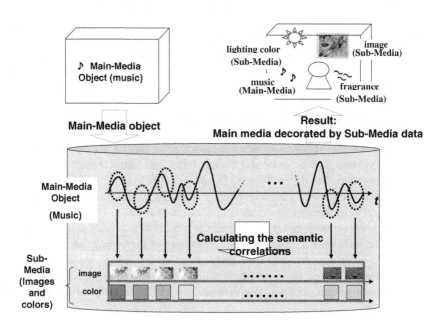

Fig. 1.5 Music decoration with images by automatic decorative-multimedia creation

「Ask Me Why」   「Anna」   「I am the Walrus」   「Good Morning」

Time

Fig. 1.6 Decoration for music-collections (the Beatles music collection) with images

Step-3   maps the metadata of the music-media object to the metadata in the image-media space, by using the MS-space ("Main-media and Sub-media transmission space"). In this step, we apply a main-media and sub-media transformation space by using the relationships between the features of music and those of images in colors, which are created by artists and psychologists. This space consists of the correlations between the impression words of music and images.

Step-4   calculates semantic correlations between the music-media object and image-media objects in the "image semantic space." In this step, we apply the MMM to calculate the impression correlation between music and images.

Step-5   outputs the semantic ranking of image-media objects as the result of our semantic associative computation process, and selects image-media objects with high correlation values to the target music-media object. This step outputs the correlation values of image data in ascending order.

Step-6   renders the music-media object with the selected images as the music-media decorated with images. This step is a rendering process for music decorated with images.

1.5.2   Color-Based Impression Analysis for Video and Decoration with "Kansei" Information

We have designed an experimental system for video analysis in terms of "*Kansei*" information expressed by the color-impression [17]. This system realizes a color-based impression analysis for video-media. This system creates a story-line in impressions by analyzing colors in each frame composing a video stream.

In this system, we have created the color-impression space using 120 chromatic colors and 10 monochrome colors defined in the "Theory of Colours" [2] and

| | 130 Basic Colors | | | | | |
	R/V	R/S	R/B	R/P	…	N/9.5
cs1	1	0	0	0	…	0
cs2	0.4	0	0	0	…	0
cs3	0	0	0	0	…	0
…	…	…	…	…	…	…
cs183	0	0	0	0.6	…	0

(183 Color-Schemas)

Fig. 1.7 Image-media features in 183 color-schema (183 impression word sets) related to 130 color variations

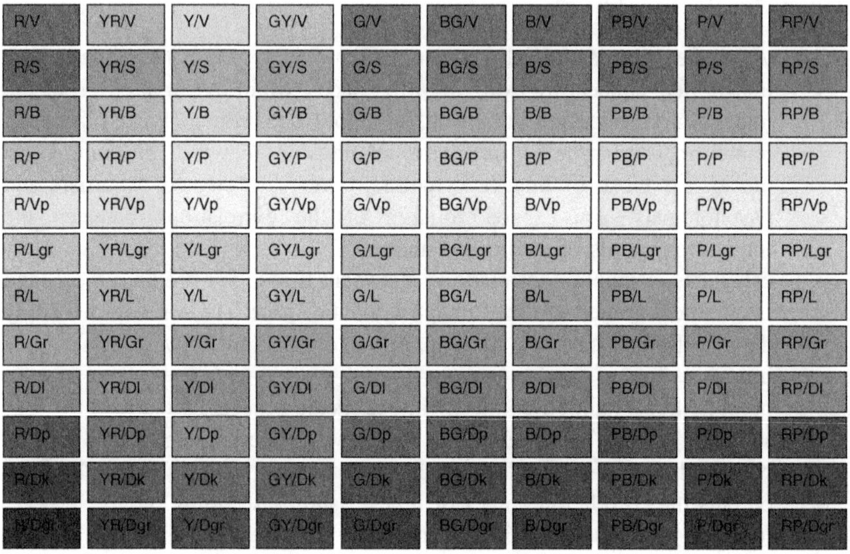

R/V	YR/V	Y/V	GY/V	G/V	BG/V	B/V	PB/V	P/V	RP/V
R/S	YR/S	Y/S	GY/S	G/S	BG/S	B/S	PB/S	P/S	RP/S
R/B	YR/B	Y/B	GY/B	G/B	BG/B	B/B	PB/B	P/B	RP/B
R/P	YR/P	Y/P	GY/P	G/P	BG/P	B/P	PB/P	P/P	RP/P
R/Vp	YR/Vp	Y/Vp	GY/Vp	G/Vp	BG/Vp	B/Vp	PB/Vp	P/Vp	RP/Vp
R/Lgr	YR/Lgr	Y/Lgr	GY/Lgr	G/Lgr	BG/Lgr	B/Lgr	PB/Lgr	P/Lgr	RP/Lgr
R/L	YR/L	Y/L	GY/L	G/L	BG/L	B/L	PB/L	P/L	RP/L
R/Gr	YR/Gr	Y/Gr	GY/Gr	G/Gr	BG/Gr	B/Gr	PB/Gr	P/Gr	RP/Gr
R/Dl	YR/Dl	Y/Dl	GY/Dl	G/Dl	BG/Dl	B/Dl	PB/Dl	P/Dl	RP/Dl
R/Dp	YR/Dp	Y/Dp	GY/Dp	G/Dp	BG/Dp	B/Dp	PB/Dp	P/Dp	RP/Dp
R/Dk	YR/Dk	Y/Dk	GY/Dk	G/Dk	BG/Dk	B/Dk	PB/Dk	P/Dk	RP/Dk
R/Dgr	YR/Dgr	Y/Dgr	GY/Dgr	G/Dgr	BG/Dgr	B/Dgr	PB/Dgr	P/Dgr	RP/Dgr

Fig. 1.8 Munsell 130 basic colors for extracting color schemas in impressions

"Color Image Scale" [19] based on the Munsell color system. We used 183 words, which are also defined as cognitive scales of colors in the Color Image Scale, as impression words in the process of construction of color-impression space, shown in Fig. 1.7. To generate a color histogram of each frame composing video, we used 130 colors in Fig. 1.8, the same number of colors used in the color-impression space. This system converts RGB values to HSV values per pixel of each image, clusters them into the closest color of 130 colors, and calculates the percentage of each color to all pixels of the image [4, 5]. The 183 color-schemas, which correspond to 183 impression word sets, are defined as color-impression variations by using the 130 basic color features, as shown in Fig. 1.7. By correlation calculations between 183 color schemas (183 impression word sets) and 130 basic colors, this system extracts the color-impression for each frame composing a video, and creates

| | 183 Color-Schemas | | | | |
	cs1	cs2	cs3	...	cs$_m$
t1	0.2	0.4	0.2	...	0.1
t2	0.1	0.1	0.0	...	0.2
t3	0.1	0.3	0.25	...	0.4
...	...	...	...	...	...
t$_n$	0.43	0.33	0.11	...	0.04

(left label: Time)

Fig. 1.9 The video-media story expressed in 183 color schema (183 impression word sets) along the timeline

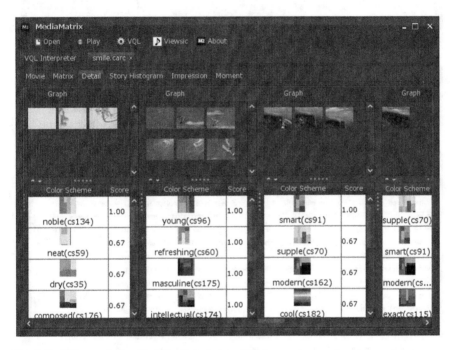

Fig. 1.10 Video analysis with 183 color-schemas (183 impression word sets) in each scene

a sequence of color-impressions of the video along the timeline, as shown in Figs. 1.9, 1.10 and 1.11 [17].

In the color-impression space used as the main-media space, this system creates a sequence of color-impressions of the video and applies it to decorate the video with sub-media, such as music or images, by using the semantic associative computation method in MMM.

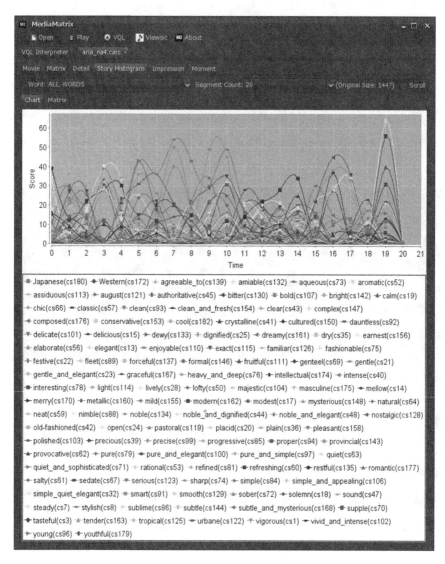

Fig. 1.11 Video-media decoration with impression-transition in color schemas (183 impression word sets) along the timeline

1.6 Cross-Cultural Computing System for Images

In this section, we present a cross-cultural computing system for images. We have proposed a method to treat culture-dependent colors by color space transformations, and analyze the color diversity and the semantics in a concept-level [1, 13, 20, 21].

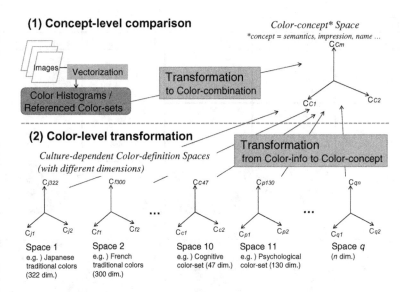

(1) Concept-level comparison

Color-concept* Space

*concept = semantics, impression, name ...

C Cm

Images — Vectorization

Transformation to Color-combination

Color Histograms / Referenced Color-sets

C C1   C C2

(2) Color-level transformation

Transformation from Color-info to Color-concept

Culture-dependent Color-definition Spaces (with different dimensions)

C j322   C f300   C c47   C p130   C qn

C j1   C j2   C f1   C f2   C c1   C c2   C p1   C p2   C q1   C q2

Space 1
e.g.) Japanese traditional colors (322 dim.)

Space 2
e.g.) French traditional colors (300 dim.)

Space 10
e.g.) Cognitive color-set (47 dim.)

Space 11
e.g.) Psychological color-set (130 dim.)

Space q
(n dim.)

Fig. 1.12 Basic method of two-level comparison in cross-cultural image computing using color space transformation

The main feature of our method is characterized as a two-level comparison: (1) Concept-level comparison and (2) Color-level space transformation (Fig. 1.12).

First, the color definitions of culture-dependent color spaces with different dimensions are set as cultural determinants to analyze (Fig. 1.13). Second, the color definitions are transformed to color-concepts to be mapped onto a color-concept

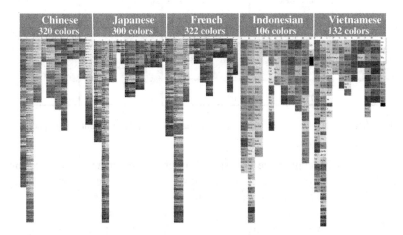

| Chinese 320 colors | Japanese 300 colors | French 322 colors | Indonesian 106 colors | Vietnamese 132 colors |

Fig. 1.13 Examples of color definitions of culture-dependent color spaces with different dimensions (traditional color sets): Chinese, French and Japanese color sets are excerpted from DIC Color Guide, and Indonesian and Vietnamese colors are collected by native color specialists

Html Color	Japan	France	Indonesia	Vietnam
Sky blue	空色 Sora-iro	Bleu Ciel	Biru Cakrawala	Xanh da trời
0.475	0.7	0.12	0.602	0.112
0.399	0.597	0.046	0.585	0.035
0.391	0.586	0.033	0.572	0.033
0.384	0.579	0.031	0.566	0.007
0.383	0.571	0.021	0.566	0.007

Fig. 1.14 Image retrieval by color name *Sky blue* in each culture-dependent color space

space. The color-concept space is a space to define the semantics, impression or names of color in a concept-level. Third, the target images are vectorized as color histograms or reference color-sets to be mapped onto the same color-concept space. Finally, the images and color-associated terms are comparable.

Our method allows comparing cultural differences and similarities using color information of image data in the concept level, which cannot be compared in color-level comparison.

Indonesian Art Paintings	Japanese	Chinese	French	Indonesian	Vietnamese
	利休鼠(0.871)	庭院瓦灰色(0.866)	SOURIS(0.908)	Oranye Rempah-Rempah(0.465)	Xám (0.885)
	消炭色(0.238)	墨緑(0.277)	MACADAM(0.199)	Hijau Puteri Malu(0.281)	ghi(0.218)
	生壁色(0.109)	黄驢色 (0.046)	BOULEAU(0.102)	Hijau Rumput(0.169)	màu cát(0.129)
	錆浅葱(0.040)	荷茎緑 (0.013)	VERT-DE-GRIS (0.066)	Ungu Torenia(0.045)	Xanh crôm (0.039)
	藤 色(0.001)	百草霜(0.008)	GRIS BLEU(0.006)	Ungu Mawar(0.031)	Đồng (0.001)

Fig. 1.15 Examples of color name extraction for Indonesian art paintings using culture-dependent traditional color sets

By automatic association of image data with the culture-dependent color diversity and the semantics, the upward scaling of image retrieval becomes possible (Fig. 1.14). Also, the representative color names of each image are able to be extracted incrementally after mapping the color distribution information of target image data to a color-concept space, because our system represents images by traditional color names through color-concept space, and a traditional color name is considered as a unit vector in the traditional color distribution space (Fig. 1.15). As mapped in the same concept-color space, the differences and common features of images are able to be compared, and the differences in language and perception are highlighted and realized as cultural differences and similarities more deeply by our method.

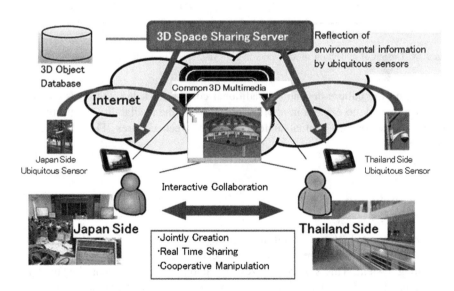

Fig. 1.16 3D cyber space museum for art work

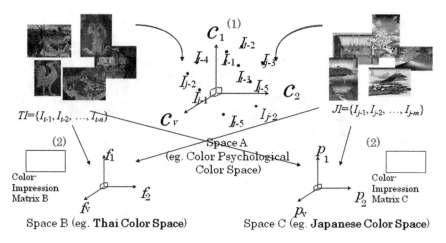

Fig. 1.17 The concept of 3D cyber space museum with Japanese and Thai images

e.g. Context="mysterious"

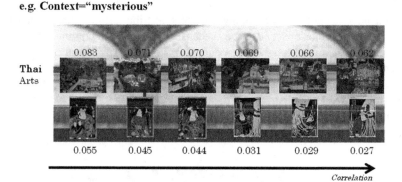

Fig. 1.18 Design of allocation of art works in 3D cyber space museum

By using the culture-dependent traditional color knowledge, the cross-cultural computing is able to expand in application based on the availability of an image's expression and deepen mutual understanding between cultures (Figs. 1.16, 1.17 and 1.18).

1.7 Conclusion

We have presented "*Kansei*-Multimedia Computing System" for realizing international and cross-cultural research environments, as a new platform of multimedia computing system. This system realizes an "automatic media decoration model" with semantic spaces and media-decoration functions for semantic associative computations for images, music and video. This paper has also presented the 3D Cyber Space Museum for Art work, as an international and cross-cultural research environment with Spatio-temporal and semantic analyzers applied to cross-cultural multimedia computing.

As our future work, we realize new cross-cultural computing environments with automatic decorative-multimedia creation among various media resources existing in different cultures based on the concept of "Opera of Meaning [22]." We also design automatic decorative-multimedia creation systems for dynamic video representation decorated with various media data.

Acknowledgments We would like to thank Prof. Takashi Kitagawa (University of Tsukuba) as a co-designer of the Mathematical Model of Meaning (MMM). We would also like to express special thanks to Prof. Shlomo Dubnov (University of California, San Diego) for his suggestive and creative discussions, and to our MDBL project members in Keio University at SFC, for valuable multimedia database system creation and experiments.

References

1. Kiyoki Y, Chen X (2009) A semantic associative computation method for automatic decorative multimedia creation with "*Kansei*" information, Invited paper. In: The Sixth Asia-Pacific conference on conceptual modelling (APCCM 2009), p 9
2. Goethe WJ (1982) Theory of colours. trans. Charles Lock Eastlake, Cambridge, Massachusetts, The M.I.T. Press
3. Harada A (eds) (1997) Report of modeling the evaluation structure of KANSEI. University of Tsukuba
4. Kiyoki Y, Kitagawa T, Hayama T (1994) A metadatabase system for semantic image search by a mathematical model of meaning. ACM Sigmod Record 23(4):34–41
5. Kiyoki Y, Kitagawa T, Hayama T (1998) A metadatabase system for semantic image search by a mathematical model of meaning. In: Sheth A, Klas W (eds) Multimedia data management—using metadata to integrate and apply digital media. McGrawHill(book) Chapter 7
6. Hofstede GH, Hofstede GJ (2005) Cultures and organizations: software of the mind. McGraw-Hill Professional
7. Cross I (2001) Music, cognition, culture and evolution. Ann N Y Acad Sci 930:28–42
8. Le MH (1999) The role of music in second language learning: a vietnamese perspective. In: For presentation at combined 1999 conference of the australian association for research in education and the New Zealand association for research in education
9. Brown N (2000) Evolutionary models of music: from sexual selection to group to group selection, Perspectives in ethology. Plenum Publishers, New York, pp 231–281
10. Trang NN, Sasaki S, Kiyoki Y (2011) A Cross-cultual music museum system with impression-based analyzing functions. In: Proceedings of IADIS e-Society 2011 conference, Avila, Spain, p 8, March 2011
11. Kitagawa T, Kiyoki Y (2001) Fundamental framework for media data retrieval systems using media-lexico transformation operator in the case of musical MIDI data. Inf Model Knowle Bases XII (IOS Press)
12. Hevner K (1936) Experimental studies of the elements of expression in music. Am J Psychol 48:246–268
13. Kiyoki Y (2000) A semantic associative search method for WWW information resources. In: Proceedings of 1st international conference on web information systems engineering (WISE2000), invited paper

14. Ijichi A, Kiyoki Y (2005) A kansei metadata generation method for music data dealing with dramatic interpretation. Inf Model Knowl Bases XVI:170–182 (IOS Press)
15. Imai S, Kurabayashi S, Kiyoki Y (2006) A music retrieval system supporting intuitive visualization by the color sense of tonality. In: Proceedings of the 24th IASTED international multi-conference databases and applications (DBA2006), pp 153–159
16. Barakbah AR, Kiyoki Y (2009) A pillar algorithm for K-means optimization by distance maximization for initial centroid designation. In: Proceedings of the IEEE international symposium on computational intelligence and data mining (CIDM). Nashville-Tennessee, USA, pp 61–68
17. Kurabayashi S, Kiyoki Y (2010) MediaMatrix: a video stream retrieval system with mechanisms for mining contexts of query examples. In: Proceedings 15th international conference on database systems for advanced applications (DASFAA2010), pp 452–455
18. Yara F, Yoshida N, Sasaki S, Kiyoki Y (2006) A continuous media data rendering system for visualizing psychological impression-transition. In: The 10th IASTED international conference on internet and multimedia systems and applications (IMSA2006), pp 32–40, Aug 2006
19. Kobayashi S (1992) Color image scale. (The Nippon Color & Design Research Institute ed., translated by Louella Matsunaga, Kodansha International
20. Nguyen TND, Sasaki S, Kiyoki Y (2011) 5D world picmap: imagination-based image search system with spatiotemporal analyzers. Proceedings of IADIS e-Society 2011 conference, Avila, Spain, p 8
21. Sasaki S, Itabashi Y, Nguyen DTN, Kiyoki Y, Barakbah AR, Takano K (2012) Cross-cultural image database system with impression-based color arrangement. In: The 1st Indonesian-Japanese conference on knowledge creation and intelligent computing (KCIC 2012), p 8, Surabaya, Indonesia, 13–14th March 2012
22. Dubnov S, Kiyoki Y (2009) Opera of meaning: film and music performance with semantic associative search. Inf Model Knowle Bases XX:384–391

Chapter 2
Cross-Cultural Aesthetics: Analyses and Experiments in Verbal and Visual Arts

Abstract Aesthetics arise from arousal of the senses followed by appraisals that make sense of what was sensed. The underlying psychology of sense-making can be modeled mathematically as a reduction in entropy, from the initial entropy of arousal to residual entropy after appraisal. This theoretical framework is applied here to the aesthetics of verbal and visual arts across American and Japanese cultures. First, a computational model is proposed to analyze the aesthetics of humor in haiku form and amusing advertisements known as Burma-Shave jingles. These analyses demonstrate how aesthetic experiences can be computed in terms of entropy reduction, for both forms of verse. Then, an experimental study is performed to characterize preferences for complexity in abstract art across samples of American and Japanese populations. This experiment further illustrates how aesthetics can be computed in terms of entropy, establishing commonalities between the two cultures and uncovering differences in aesthetic preferences of individuals.

2.1 A Theoretical Framework for Computing Aesthetics

Aesthetics are often attributed to *"unity in variety"* [7, 9, 25, 27–29]—where unity refers to some measure of order, regularity, symmetry, or harmony; and variety refers to some measure of chaos, irregularity, asymmetry, or complexity. More formally, a number of authors have offered mathematical measures of unity and variety, along with equations for how these two factors are combined to compute aesthetics [6, 8, 23, 31, 37, 45]. Unfortunately, most of these equations are lacking a psychological foundation and empirical validation.

One alternative is a recent theory dubbed EVE′, which models the aesthetic experience mathematically in terms of psychological expectations (E), violations (V) of expectations, and explanations (E′) of violations. Formal analyses and human experiments have established that EVE′ can explain and predict aspects of aesthetics in verbal, visual, and musical media [10–14].

This initial section of the chapter compares EVE′ to other theories of aesthetics, in order to establish key differences and equivalences. In particular, EVE′ is shown

© The Author(s) 2016   21
S. Dubnov et al., *Cross-Cultural Multimedia Computing*,
SpringerBriefs in Computer Science, DOI 10.1007/978-3-319-42873-4_2

to be similar to another equation that quantifies the audience's experience as an information rate (IR) in signal processing [17–19]. Then subsequent sections of the chapter apply EVE′ to analyses and experiments in verbal and visual arts. The results of these studies offer insights into universal aspects of aesthetics across American and Japanese cultures, as well as personal preferences of individuals within each culture.

2.1.1 Birkhoff and Bense

Arguably the first formal theory of aesthetics was offered by George Birkhoff [8] as an equation that expressed his notion of *"unity in variety"*. Birkhoff's equation was $M = O/C$, where O is order, C is complexity, and M is a measure of aesthetics obtained from order (unity) in complexity (variety). Over the years this equation has been influential among scientists attempting to model aesthetics [6, 7, 20, 22–24, 29, 31, 32, 35, 37, 40, 45], despite some important limitations.

Birkhoff's equation was based only on personal introspection, without any psychological foundation or empirical validation to support the assumed relation between M, O, and C. For example, Hutcheson's [27, 45] notion of *"unity in variety"* implies an equation $M = O * C$, as proposed by Eysenck [23], as opposed to $M = O/C$. And actually empirical testing reviewed by Eysenck [22, 24] shows that $M = O * C$ offers a better match to psychological judgments of aesthetics than $M = O/C$. But a limitation of both equations lies in how the factors O and C are quantified. Birkhoff himself proposed only ad hoc methods for computing O and C from features of artworks, and neither he nor subsequent researchers ever tested those methods against human judgments of order and complexity. As a result, failure of Birkhoff's M to match human judgments of aesthetics could be attributed to the equation $M = O/C$, or to methods by which an experimenter computes values of O and C needed as input to this equation.

Several decades after Birkhoff, other scientists led by Max Bense [6, 32, 40] used concepts from Shannon's theory of communication [42] to more formally compute the factors O and C. In particular, Bense assumed that complexity (C) could be quantified by Shannon's entropy (H), which measures the information in a set of signals. This entropy is computed as $H = \Sigma_i P_i * -\log P_i$, where P_i is the probability (frequency) at which a signal s_i occurs and the sum is taken over the set of all signals $\{s_i\}$ in an artwork. The term $-\log P_i$, known as *surprisal* [15, 42], is a positive quantity that increases as P decreases. That is, an improbable signal s_i with low P_i and high $-\log P_i$ will be *surprising* when it is received. Therefore, Shannon's entropy H can be characterized as a weighted-average surprisal across all signals in an artwork, with surprisal $-\log P_i$ for each signal s_i weighed by the frequency P_i at which that signal appears in the artwork.

Several models are attributed to Bense and his contemporaries, but these models all assume Birkhoff's equation and differ only in how the factors O and C are quantified. One model [37] is $O = H_{max} - H$, $C = H_{max}$, and $M = 1 - H/H_{max}$, where H_{max} is the maximum value of entropy that occurs when all signals in the set $\{s_i\}$ are equally probable. For a given set of possible signals, H_{max} is a constant such that M increases as H decreases. Another model [32] is $O = (H_{max} - H)/H_{max}$, $C = H$, and $M = 1/H - 1/H_{max}$. This model also predicts that M increases as H decreases, such that aesthetics M would be maximized when entropy H is minimized.

2.1.2 IR and EVE'

More recently, principles of information theory have been used to derive an expression [17–19] known as *information rate* (IR). Unlike Bense's formulation, which is concerned with a compositional set of signals that comprise an artwork (e.g., an image), IR is concerned with a temporal sequence of signals received by an audience (e.g., in music). Also unlike Bense's formulation, IR does not adopt Birkhoff's equation $M = O/C$. Instead IR computes a measure of aesthetics as mutual information, between a signal without any past context and the same signal given its past context. This mutual information is a difference between two entropies, $IR = H - H'$, where: $H = -\log P(signal)$ is the entropy of a signal *independent* of past signals; and $H' = -\log P(signal|past\ signals)$ is the entropy of the same signal *in the context* of past signals.

Other authors [3, 31, 45] have also argued that aesthetics involve a reduction in entropy. Indeed, Bense himself had this idea [40] in a model written as $M = O/C = (H_1 - H_2)/H_1$, where H_1 is an entropy computed from symbols that encode the stimulus, and H_2 is an entropy computed from super-symbols that re-code the stimulus. But IR differs in its approach to compression, by computing the entropy of a signal in the context of past signals.

Further insight into IR as a model of aesthetics can be gained by examining the underlying psychological processes of *arousal* and *appraisal* [7, 21, 33, 34, 41, 43, 44]. This perspective is promoted by the theory of EVE' [10–14], which models mental expectations (E), violations (V) of expectations, and explanations (E') of violations. EVE's equation for aesthetics is $X = Y * Z$, where: Y models arousal from the violation of an expectation (i.e., the V of E); and Z models appraisal from an explanation of the violation (i.e., the E' of V). Mathematically, Y is computed via information theory [15, 42] as the marginal entropy of a signal that is received, $-\log P(signal)$; and Z is computed via Bayesian theory [5, 30] as the posterior probability of the meaning that most likely *explains* the signal that was received, $P(meaning|signal)$.

As outlined above, EVE's aesthetic measure X is expressed as the product of an entropy and probability, whereas IR's aesthetic measure is expressed as a difference between two entropies. But an equivalence exists if one assumes that the context provided by past signals can *explain* the meaning of a present signal. Using H to denote the marginal entropy $-\log P(signal)$ that quantifies a violation of expectation, and using Q to denote the posterior probability $P(meaning|signal)$ that quantifies explanation of the violation, EVE's product of arousal and appraisal is $X = Y * Z = H * Q$. An equivalence to IR is then seen by rewriting the equation as follows: $X = H - H * (1 - Q) = H - H' = IR$.

In this equation, H represents the magnitude of initial surprise experienced as arousal, and $H' = H * (1 - Q)$ represents the magnitude of residual surprise *not explained* in appraisal. Thus H' and $H * (1 - Q)$ are merely different ways of computing how much surprise has been experienced and *not explained*. So both IR and EVE' are measuring *how much surprise has been experienced and explained*.

Now returning to the equations of Birkhoff-Bense, we can distinguish an important difference from IR-EVE'. This is seen most easily from EVE's formulation $X = Y * Z$, where marginal entropy $Y = -\log P(signal)$ is a measure of complexity akin to C, and posterior probability $Z = P(meaning|signal)$ is a measure of order akin to O. By substitution, EVE's equation can be rewritten as $X = C * O$, which is equivalent to Eysenck's equation $M = O * C$ and different from the Birkhoff-Bense equation $M = O/C$.

2.1.3 Models of Memory

An important aspect of IR, as it relates to EVE', is the idea that past signals can explain the meaning of a present signal. Here one might wonder: If past signals (which have just been received prior to the present signal) are capable of *explaining* the present signal, then why were these same past signals not capable of *expecting* the present signal? In other words, if past signals can *reduce* surprise by an amount $H - H'$, then why do these past signals not *prevent* the same amount of surprise from occurring in the first place?

Here the psychological perspective of EVE' offers insight by modeling two types of memory involved in expectations (E) and explanations (E'), respectively. First, *expectations* (and violations of expectations) are governed by representations of meanings and signals held in *working memory*. The working memory of humans is known to be quite limited [4, 16], such that only a handful of so-called "chunks" are able to hold possible meanings and potential signals. On the other hand, *explanations* are based on extremely rich associations between meanings and signals that are represented in *long-term memory*.

In effect, the explanation of a present signal by past signals is a *re-cognition*—whereby associations between present and past signals are recalled from long-term memory *only after* the present signal is actually received and represented (along with past signals) in working memory. Therefore, past signals can be effective in explaining a present signal (via long-term memory), after it has been received; whereas past signals are less effective in expecting the same signal (via working memory), before it has been received. This difference in effectiveness, due to different memory systems, helps account for how past signals *can explain* but *not expect* a subsequent signal in a sequence of signals.

The nature of long-term memory also offers insight into EVE's notion of *meaning*, and IR's assumption that past signals can *explain* a present signal. That is, re-cognition entails associations between the present signal and past signals as these signals are all represented in long-term memory. But long-term memory also extends far beyond signals to include associated knowledge at a higher level of abstraction—which EVE' refers to as *meaning*. Thus together the past and present signals held in working memory will *evoke* associated meanings via long-term memory, and these evoked meanings (rather than past signals per se) are what actually *explain* the present signal.

This conceptual difference between *signals* and *meanings* is important for two reasons. First, explanations of signals (data) require associations to meaning (knowledge) at a higher level of abstraction, because signals at one level of abstraction cannot really *explain* other signals at the same level of abstraction. Second, the co-occurrence statistics of signals within artworks are often not sufficient to compute the higher-level semantics of meaning needed to *explain* signals. A specific example is provided in the next section, which uses EVE' to analyze the aesthetics of poetic verse.

2.2 A Computational Model of Verbal Aesthetics

In the domain of verbal arts, EVE' has been used to explain and predict aesthetics for two types of short verse. These two types were chosen to control for variables such as the total length of a verse and the grouping of words in lines, which can affect judgments of complexity and aesthetics. One type is haiku, a well-known form in Japanese tradition but also written in many other languages including English [1, 2, 26, 36, 38, 46]. The other type is rhyming "jingles", used by an American company to advertise their shaving cream called Burma-Shave [39]. For both forms of verse, the aesthetic of interest here is one of humorous amusement.

2.2.1 Haiku Humor

In Japan, humor in haiku form is often referred to as *senryu*, after the name of a poet who popularized this comic genre in the 1700s. But outside Japan the term haiku is used more broadly, and in English all poems structured in three lines with $5 + 7 + 5 = 17$ syllables are properly referred to as haiku [36]. The following is an example that illustrates the theory of EVE':

an apple a day

will keep the doctor away

said devil to Eve

In analyzing this example [11], each line can be considered a signal received in temporal sequence as the verse is read. But besides these three *signals* (s_1, s_2, s_3) that serve as *evidence*, an analysis must also consider the *meanings* that an audience entertains as *hypotheses* to explain the signals. For example, after the first two lines a reader will think it is very likely that the verse is referring to a well-known proverb about how apples are healthy and hence good to eat. So after s_1 and s_2, but before s_3, the reader will be thinking $P(A|s_1,s_2)$ = high and $P(\sim A|s_1,s_2)$ = low, where: A = "apples are good to eat" is a hypothesized meaning associated with the well-known proverb; and $\sim A$ is a catch-all hypothesis that includes other possible but unspecified meanings of the verse.

Although many specific meanings may be represented in long-term memory and used to *explain* signals, only a small set like {A, $\sim A$} can be retained in working memory and used to *expect* the next signal. So with $P(A|s_1,s_2)$ = high, a reader will expect the next signal s_3 to be in class "a" consistent with A = "apples are good to eat", such that $P(a|s_1,s_2)$ = high and $P(\sim a|s_1,s_2)$ = low. Once again, notice that only a small set {a, $\sim a$} of potential signals is represented in working memory and used to *expect* the next signal.

Finally, after expecting a signal s_3 = "a", the experienced signal is actually s_3 = "$\sim a$". That is, the last line of the verse refers to characters in the context of a bible story where apples are bad to eat, which is inconsistent with A = "apples are good to eat". This experience of s_3 (after s_2 and s_1) produces a high violation of expectation, or *arousal*, which can be quantified as $Y = -\log P(\sim a|s_1,s_2)$ = high. The arousal, in turn, sparks a search through long-term memory for some meaning that can explain the signal, in a process of *appraisal* to "make sense" of the surprise.

A reader who "gets it" will realize that the meaning of the verse is not A but B, where B = "apples are bad to eat and the devil is using the proverb as a way to tempt Eve". Notice that B comes from background knowledge about bible stories and the devil's intent to deceive Adam and Eve in the Garden of Eden. This knowledge (recalled from long-term memory) is not contained in signals of the verse itself, because none of the signals makes mention of any individual's aims or intentions. But based on a reader's background knowledge, the meaning B makes sense of the surprising signal s_3 after previous signals s_2 and s_1, so the Bayesian posterior probability is $P(B|s_1,s_2,s_3)$ = high.

Finally, EVE' computes the magnitude of aesthetic experience as X = Y * Z, where $Y = -\log P(\sim a|s_1,s_2)$ = high and $Z = P(B|s_1,s_2,s_3)$ = high. This yields X = high, so the haiku is humorous to those who experience and understand it.

In contrast, consider two alternative endings that yield low X, one due to low Y and the other due to low Z. For the first case, assume s_3 = "said the old proverb". Here we have little surprise (arousal), because s_3 is in class "a" consistent with A, so s_3 is expected after s_1 and s_2. The resulting verse makes sense (high Z), but X = Y * Z is low because Y is low. For the second case, assume s_3 = "said postman to Eve". Here we have little meaning (appraisal), because background knowledge offers no apparent reason for a postman to be reciting the apple proverb to Eve (of bible fame, or other Eve). So s_3 may be surprising (high Y), but X = Y * Z is low because Z is low.

As described above, a high aesthetic X requires both high surprise Y and high meaning Z together. Now with respect to IR, this same product Y * Z might be modeled as an entropy difference H − H′, where: H = −log $P(s_3|s_1,s_2)$ = high, to model the initial surprise experienced before explanation of s_3; and H′ = −log $P(s_3|s_1,s_2, B)$ = low, to model the residual surprise remaining after explanation of s_3. But notice the context B that explains the signal s_3 is not past signals (s_1 and s_2) themselves, because the past signals were received before s_3, and actually these past signals need to be explained along with the present signal in order to make sense of the verse. Instead the context that explains s_3 (and s_2 and s_1) is an associated meaning B at a higher level of abstraction. This meaning is *re-cognized* only after all three signals (s_1, s_2, and s_3) are received and have evoked long-term memories of the apple proverb and bible story. In fact, re-cognition involves *re-combination* of these memories, in *creation* of an explanation for the novel situation (i.e., devil reciting the apple proverb) that was not previously stored in long-term memory.

This example illustrates commonalities as well as a key difference between IR and EVE′. A common aspect of both approaches is to quantify surprise in terms of entropy, denoted H in IR and Y in EVE′. The difference then comes in computing how this surprise is explained or not by an audience. IR models the amount of surprise that is *not explained by past signals*, via the term H′ = H(signal|past signals). This makes IR applicable to artworks for which surprise can be explained by the co-occurrence statistics of signals. EVE′ models the fraction of surprise that *is explained by some meaning*, via the term Z = P(meaning|signals). This makes EVE′ applicable to other artworks, like the apple haiku, for which surprise is explained by meanings that cannot be computed from the co-occurrence statistics of signals themselves.

2.2.2   Serious Semantics

Of course not all haiku are humorous, and EVE′ also applies when the semantics are serious. As an example, consider a famous verse by Bashō:

furu ike ya

kawazu tobikomu

mizu no oto

which is translated by Addiss [1] as follows:

old pond

a frog jumps in

the sound of water

Here the first two lines describe a sight, but then the last line describes a sound—which is surprising because it involves "sense-switching" [36]. The surprise is explained by combining sight and sound into a coherent re-cognition of the familiar frog-pond scene, based on long-term memories of natural experiences. As such, the aesthetic arises from meaning assigned to signals that initially appear incongruous but eventually are found harmonious.

Thus like high amusement for humorous haiku, high aesthetics for serious haiku are the product of high surprise (Y) and high meaning (Z). And once again, the meaning assigned to signals comes not from signals contained within the artwork itself—but rather from common knowledge shared by a culture of artists and audiences who live in the same natural world.

In today's state of the art, it remains an unsolved challenge for artificial intelligence to model the meanings that humans assign to signals as they experience artworks. In language if not other media, this requires rich representations of human knowledge about the real world—including hypothetical meanings of evidential signals, along with prior probabilities of the form P(meaning) and conditional probabilities of the form P(signal|meaning). These representations are needed to compute the marginal probability of a signal across the set of possible meanings in *working memory*, P(signal) = Σ P(meaning) * P(signal|meaning), in EVE's factor Y = −log P(signal). They are also needed to compute posterior probabilities of possible meanings from *long-term memory*, P(meaning|signal) = P(meaning) * P(signal|meaning)/P(signal), for EVE's factor Z = P(meaning|signal).

In short, models of *meanings* for signals are required if artificial intelligence is to credibly compute aesthetic experiences—which are governed by how much surprise is experienced and *explained*.

2.2.3 Amusing Advertisements

Unfortunately, the needed knowledge structures are not currently available from artificial intelligence. As a consequence, it is not feasible to compute EVE's factors Y and Z from first principles, at least not for narrative or figurative arts in which rich semantics are involved. But EVE' can still be applied to these arts by asking humans for their judgments of meaning (Z) and surprise (Y), from which aesthetics (X) can be computed as X = Y * Z. The model-predicted values of X can then be compared to human-reported judgments of aesthetics, as a test of EVE's equation X = Y * Z.

This approach was applied [13] in a study of advertising jingles made famous by the Burma-Shave company [39]. These jingles are similar to haiku in that they have a fixed form and short length. More specifically, each jingle is written in five lines with a total number of syllables similar to the 17 of haiku. In Burma-Shave's original advertising campaign, each line of a jingle was painted on a separate sign and the signs were spaced along roadways so that readers in vehicles would experience a several-second delay between lines. An example is the following verse:

he's the boy

the gals forgot

his line

was smooth

his chin was not

A total of 20 prototypical jingles were chosen from among 600 published verses [39] originally used as advertisements by the Burma-Shave company. These 20 jingles were then presented in a survey [13] that asked human participants to make three judgments (on a scale of 1 to 5) for each jingle. The judgments were answers to the following three questions: *Did you understand the verse? Did the ending surprise you? Was the jingle creative?* At the end of the survey, all participants strongly or very strongly agreed that their judgments of creativeness were based on feelings of amusement. Thus answers to the three questions provide direct measures of EVE's variables Z (meaning), Y (surprise), and X (pleasure), respectively.

The data collected by this survey were used to compute average values of Z, Y, and X across all participants (N = 81), for each jingle. The average human values of Y and Z were then used to compute aesthetic predictions for five models: $X = Y * Z$; $X = Z/Y$; $X = Y/Z$; $X = Y$; and $X = Z$. Notice that the first model $X = Y * Z$ is EVE's equation and analogous to Eysenck's equation $M = C * O$, whereas the second model $X = Z/Y$ is analogous to the equation $M = O/C$ of Birkhoff and Bense.

These model-predicted values of X were compared to the human-reported (average) values of X for all 20 jingles. The results [13] showed that EVE's model $X = Y * Z$ was by far the best, with model-predicted X accounting for a remarkable 70 % of the variation in human-reported X across jingles. The Birkhoff-Bense model $X = Z/Y$ was the worst of all five models tested. In fact, it was the only model to predict a negative correlation across jingles, where model-predicted X decreased as human-reported X increased.

These results strongly suggest that the term Y representing complexity C belongs in the numerator of $X = Y * Z$, as modeled by EVE' and Eysenck's equation $M = O * C$; rather than in the denominator, as modeled by the Birkhoff-Bense equation $M = O/C$.

2.3 An Experimental Study of Visual Aesthetics

The previous section provided empirical support for EVE's equation $X = Y * Z$ over other mathematical models of aesthetic experience. However, testing required human judgments of Y and Z as input to the equation, and a more thorough test of EVE' would compute Y and Z directly from first principles.

As noted earlier, computing Y and Z from first principles requires detailed models of human knowledge that are not currently available from artificial intelligence. This knowledge of *meaning* extends far beyond the data in *signals* comprising artworks themselves. But for some forms of art, it appears that the magnitude of an explanation can be estimated—at least to a first approximation—without explicitly modeling the meanings by which signals are explained.

One example is in music, where IR uses the associative context provided by past signals to explain present signals, without an explicit model of meaning. Using this approach, empirical testing of two contemporary music compositions [18, 19] showed that IR could predict 20–40 % of the variation in human judgments for "emotional force", as measured continuously while subjects listened to these compositions. Another example is abstract art [12], which is analyzed by EVE′ and empirically tested below. Abstract art is much like music, and unlike other visual or verbal media, because the features (signals) of an abstract design do not represent objects (meanings) outside the artwork itself.

2.3.1 Abstract Artworks

In the realm of abstract art, a constrained form of composition using only vertical and horizontal grid lines [12] was used to simplify the analysis of semantics in EVE's factor Z. For these artworks, it is reasonable to assume that the meaning assigned to signals (i.e., grid lines and shapes) is one of overall *coherence* (i.e., order or balance) that characterizes the composition. With this assumption, Z (coherence) can be modeled as an inverse function of Y (complexity): $Z = (Y_{max} - Y)/Y_{max}$. Notice that this is basically the same assumption as we saw earlier in a model by one of Bense's contemporaries, where order was written as $O = (H_{max} - H)/H_{max}$. But for EVE′ the approach applies only to abstract art in which semantics are extremely simplified. As discussed below, the same grid-line compositions that enable use of this simplified model for Z also enable EVE's factor Y to be computed directly from the features of an artwork, without any knowledge of real-world objects outside the artwork.

Unlike IR, which models signals in a temporal and sequential fashion, an audience's processing of a visual artwork is spatial and parallel. Although such artworks are inspected in a temporal sequence via eye saccades, the resulting sequence is constrained more by the audience than by the artwork itself. Because this sequence will vary with the viewer, and because signals are received in parallel as well as sequentially, the process can be modeled as if all signals of an artwork are received together and then explained together. In that case IR equals the difference between initial entropy (of all signals) before explanation and residual entropy (of all signals) after explanation, which EVE′ models as $X = Y * Z$.

A novel aspect of EVE's approach to these artworks lies in modeling Y as a visual entropy V_E. Details are discussed in [12], but the main point here is that V_E measures spatial complexity in a manner that differs from classical entropy H. In particular, EVE′ computes visual entropy as $V_E = 1/N * \Sigma_n -\log A_n$, where the sum is taken over all N white shapes (rectangles) bounded by black lines in the grid, and

A_n represents the area of an individual white shape computed as a fraction of the total area. Thus per this V_E, total surprisal for an artwork is computed as the average surprisal across all white shapes (bounded by black lines), with surprisal for each white shape given by $-\log A_n$.

As described above, V_E depends on the number of black lines and spacing between lines, which define the number of white shapes and area of each shape, respectively. In contrast, classical entropy H is computed as $H = \Sigma_i P_i * -\log P_i$, where i refers to a pixel color (black or white) and P_i is the frequency of that pixel color in the image. Unlike V_E, H depends only on the number of grid lines in an image (of a fixed size) and not the spacing between lines, because the frequencies of black and white pixels are determined only by the number of black lines in a grid.

The experiment [12] involved five pages of designs, shown in Fig. 2.1. For each page, which presented five panels in random order across the page, human participants provided two types of rankings. First, the five panels on a page were ranked from most (rank = 5) to least (rank = 1) *visually complex*. Then, the same five panels were ranked from most (rank = 5) to least (rank = 1) *aesthetically pleasing*. For each page, the average ranking across N = 148 human participants in an American population was used to test EVE' and other models.

The human rankings for visual complexity appear in Fig. 2.2, and the human rankings for aesthetic quality appear in Fig. 2.3. The human rankings for visual complexity (Fig. 2.2) were used to test EVE's model for entropy V_E, and also to test the model of classical entropy H. The human rankings for aesthetic quality (Fig. 2.3) were used to test EVE's prediction of aesthetic optimality as a function of visual entropy. The same human rankings for aesthetic quality were also used to test the prediction of Birkhoff-Bense that M will be maximized when classical entropy H is minimized.

The human rankings for visual complexity (Fig. 2.2) showed that EVE's visual entropy V_E was a much better model than classical entropy H. Using Spearman's rank-order correlation coefficient, averaged over all five pages of the experiment, V_E scored a 98 % match to human judgments of visual complexity, whereas H scored only 60 %. The low score for H was because classical entropy depends only on the number of lines in a design, whereas human judgments are clearly sensitive to both the number of lines and the spacing between lines.

The human rankings for aesthetic quality (Fig. 2.3) showed that EVE's model X was much better than the Birkhoff-Bense measure M. Using Spearman's rank-order correlation coefficient, X scored a 91 % match to human judgments, whereas M scored only 42 %. This low score for M was because the Birkhoff-Bense model always predicts the simplest panel on a page will be ranked as most aesthetic, whereas humans typically found panels of intermediate complexity to be most aesthetic.

For example, according to EVE's equation $X = Y * Z = Y * (Y_{max} - Y)/Y_{max}$, the optimal aesthetic ($dX/dY = 0$) will occur at $Y_{opt} = Y_{max}/2$. As seen from Fig. 2.3, this prediction is generally consistent with the intermediate level of complexity found to be optimal (on average across subjects) in the experiment.

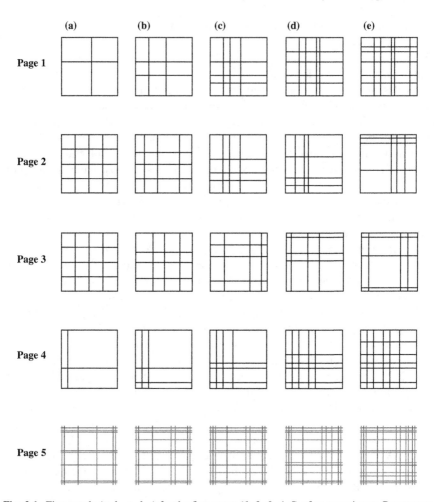

Fig. 2.1 Five panels (*a, b, c, d, e*) for the five pages (*1, 2, 3, 4, 5*) of an experiment. Pages were shown one at a time, with panels arranged in random order across the page. For each page of five panels, participants provided rankings of visual complexity and aesthetic quality

These results are noteworthy for two reasons. First, the scores show that EVE's equation for X is much better than the aesthetic measure M of Birkhoff and Bense. Second, the experiment also tested factors V_E and H that are needed as inputs to equations for X and M, respectively. Although limited to a simple domain of abstract designs, V_E and H were computed from first principles based only on the visual features of these graphic designs. [Note that human judgments of Z or O were not collected, because pilot testing showed that humans judged coherence (i.e., order or balance) as the logical opposite of complexity.] Thus unlike other attempts to test aesthetic equations of Birkhoff and Bense, this experiment tested not only the equations but also the factors that are input to those equations.

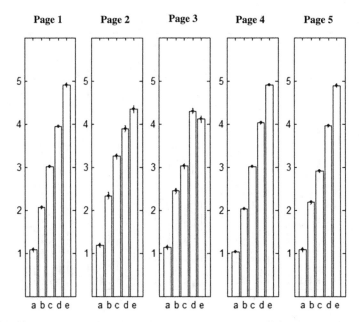

Fig. 2.2 Average human rankings of visual complexity, for five panels (a, b, c, d, e) on each page ($1, 2, 3, 4, 5$) of the experiment. Error bars represent standard errors of the mean. Data are from $N = 148$ American participants

Modeling these inputs is a matter of semantics, because *signals* like "black lines" and "white shapes" can themselves be characterized as *meanings* for lower-level signals like black and white pixels. Here instead EVE' models meaning as the overall coherence of a composition, and treats black lines and white shapes as signals. The experiment showed that visual entropy V_E captured human judgments of signal complexity, using these black lines and white shapes as signal categories; whereas classical entropy H failed to capture human judgments of signal complexity, using individual pixel colors as signal categories.

Recall that a similar situation regarding the semantics of signals arose earlier in analysis of haiku humor. That is, in theory a line of verse might be treated as the meaning for words in that line. But instead EVE' models a higher level of abstraction, where lines are considered signals in computing the meaning of a verse. The point here is that any application of a model like EVE' or IR requires assumptions about the appropriate level at which to model signals and meanings. And those assumptions are essentially semantic, because meanings at one level of abstraction can serve as signals at a higher level of abstraction.

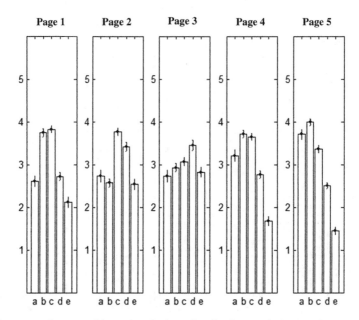

Fig. 2.3 Average human rankings of aesthetic quality, for five panels (*a, b, c, d, e*) on each page (*1, 2, 3, 4, 5*) of the experiment. Error bars represent standard errors of the mean. Data are from N = 148 American participants

2.3.2 Personal Preferences

Besides the average rankings of complexity and aesthetics used to test EVE′ and other models, individual human judgments from the experiment were used to analyze personal preferences. More specifically, the aesthetically optimal level of visual complexity C_{opt} for each participant was obtained from the rankings provided by that participant. The average value of C_{opt}, over the four pages of black-and-white designs, was then used to characterize a participant's aesthetic preference for visual complexity ranging from $C_{opt} = 1$ to $C_{opt} = 5$.

Figure 2.4 shows the results for C_{opt} across all N = 148 Americans that were tested. A total of 11 subjects had $C_{opt} = 1$, which means they always preferred the simplest design on a page. Only one subject had $C_{opt} = 5$. Most subjects had C_{opt} between 2 and 4, and the average value across all subjects was $C_{opt} = 2.76$.

As part of the study, participants were also asked to answer demographic questions about their gender (male or female), age group (<48 years or ≥ 48 years), training (some or no training in art), and taste (like or dislike abstract art). Student's t-tests were performed to compare mean values of C_{opt} for each binary distinction. Results showed that none of the demographic variables was a significant predictor of C_{opt}. Gender was the only variable that even approached significance (p = 0.08), with females having a higher C_{opt} (mean = 2.90) than males (mean = 2.64).

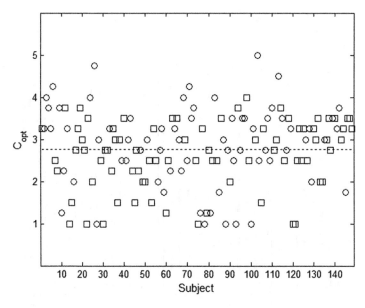

Fig. 2.4 Individual values of C_{opt}, representing each participant's aesthetically optimal level of visual complexity. C_{opt} is measured on a scale of 1–5, as an average over the first four pages of the experiment. *Squares* denote male subjects and *circles* denote female subjects. Data are from $N = 148$ American participants

These results show that aesthetic preferences for visual complexity are quite varied, even among a culture consisting of all Americans. Moreover, the individual differences are difficult to predict, even by factors such as art taste and training that would be expected to affect a person's preferences.

2.3.3 Cultural Comparison

After the above experiment with an American population, the same abstract designs were used to test a Japanese population—using verbal instructions translated into their language. Both average and individual results were analyzed.

Figures 2.5 and 2.6 show the average rankings for visual complexity and aesthetic quality across $N = 51$ Japanese participants. Qualitatively, the results are similar to those for $N = 148$ Americans presented in Figs. 2.2 and 2.3. Like the Americans, the Japanese judged visual complexity consistent with visual entropy (V_E) and found aesthetic optimality at an intermediate level of complexity.

Figure 2.7 shows the individual values of C_{opt} for Japanese participants. A comparison to American participants in Fig. 2.4 shows the distributions are similar. Although the mean value of C_{opt} is higher for Japanese (2.93) than for Americans (2.76), a t-test showed this difference was not significant.

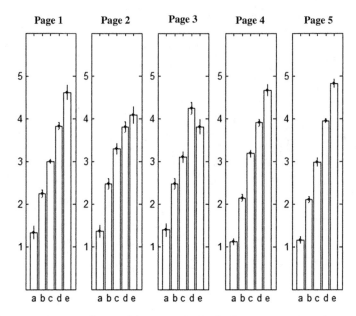

Fig. 2.5 Average human rankings of visual complexity, for five panels (*a, b, c, d, e*) on each page (*1, 2, 3, 4, 5*) of the experiment. Error bars represent standard errors of the mean. Data are from N = 51 Japanese participants

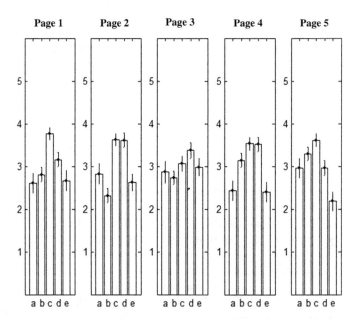

Fig. 2.6 Average human rankings of aesthetic quality, for five panels (*a, b, c, d, e*) on each page (*1, 2, 3, 4, 5*) of the experiment. Error bars represent standard errors of the mean. Data are from N = 51 Japanese participants

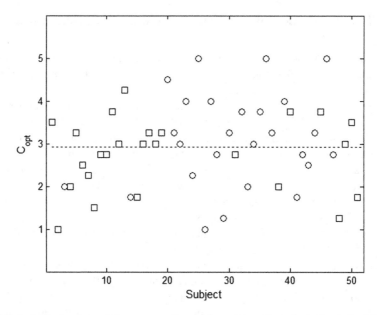

Fig. 2.7 Individual values of C_{opt}, representing each participant's aesthetically optimal level of visual complexity. C_{opt} is measured on a scale of 1–5, as an average over the first four pages of the experiment. *Squares* denote male subjects and *circles* denote female subjects. Data are from N = 51 Japanese participants

Finally, the distribution of C_{opt} within the Japanese population of participants was analyzed as a function of the same demographic variables analyzed earlier for Americans. Like the American results, mean C_{opt} was higher for females (3.10) than for males (2.74). But t-tests showed that none of the demographic variables, including gender, was significant.

It should be noted that 47 of the 51 Japanese participants were <28 years old. This demographic differs from the American survey, which included 84 participants <48 years old and 64 participants ≥ 48 years old. However, the American results showed no significant difference due to age.

In sum, the aesthetically preferred level of complexity was higher for Japanese than Americans, and higher for females than males in both cultures, but these differences were not significant. This suggests that aesthetic preferences for complexity in abstract art vary as much within a culture as between the cultures, and that preferences cannot be predicted by demographic variables such as gender, age group, training (some or no training in art), or taste (like or dislike abstract art).

2.4 The Fundamental Challenge of Computing Semantics

In conclusion, this final section of the chapter highlights what has been done and what remains to be done for artificial intelligence to credibly compute aesthetic experiences within and across cultures.

First, what has been done here is to characterize and compare several mathematical models of aesthetics. The models known as IR and EVE' were shown to be essentially equivalent, under the assumption that past signals can explain a present signal received in a temporal sequence of signals. In that case both IR and EVE' compute aesthetics as an incremental reduction in entropy, equal to *how much surprise has been experienced and explained*. This formulation by IR and EVE' was contrasted to earlier equations by Birkhoff and Bense, and tested against human judgments of aesthetics across examples of verbal and visual arts—using participants from American and Japanese populations. The results strongly support IR and EVE' over the equations of Birkhoff and Bense.

In the visual domain of abstract art, empirical testing went further to address the computation of entropy (complexity) needed as input Y to EVE's equation $X = Y * Z$. Results showed that visual entropy V_E was much better than classical entropy H as a model of how humans judge visual complexity. This highlights the importance of modeling signals at levels of abstraction consistent with those of human perception.

Next, what remains to be done for computing aesthetics lies in the problem of computing semantics. IR addresses semantics only implicitly, as signals are explained by past *signals*. EVE' addresses semantics more explicitly, as signals are explained by *meanings* evoked from long-term memory associations. However, EVE' has not encoded the vast human knowledge needed to compute these meanings and their probabilities in any specific domain.

Instead EVE' has either asked humans for their judgments of meaning (in a verbal domain); or else analyzed abstract artworks for which meaning could be modeled as a simple function of signal features (in a visual domain). This was done in the spirit of what Scha and Bod [40] suggested 20 years ago, as follows: "*For a specific, narrowly defined class of inputs (such as line drawings or grids), such a process-model [of aesthetic perception] might be worked out. But it would be absolutely out of the question to accomplish this in the context of a complete simulation of all possibilities of human visual perception. Things get even more difficult when we introduce the semantic dimension…*"

The value of models like IR and EVE' was also foreshadowed by Scha and Bod [40] as follows: "*For the time being, we cannot work out such a semantic model in any detail. But it will become more concretely imaginable as soon as a very limited purely syntactic model would show interesting results. Thus, the ultimate benefit of the computational approach to the esthetic will not lie in the models that can be implemented and validated—but in the more speculative and encompassing models which they make thinkable.*" Experiments with IR [18, 19] and EVE' [12, 13] have shown interesting and valid results—i.e., more consistent with human judgments than competing models by Birkhoff, Bense, and their followers in the field of information aesthetics [32, 37, 40]. Thus IR and EVE' may help make computational models of aesthetics more "thinkable" by artificial intelligence.

In particular, both IR and EVE' suggest that aesthetics are governed universally by *how much surprise is experienced and explained*. Mathematically, this can be modeled as a reduction in entropy, similar to "work" done in the realm of a thermodynamic system. But psychologically, which is the realm in which art "works", the amount of surprise actually experienced and explained will be determined by meanings that exist in the minds of audiences. These semantics are especially important for addressing cultural differences, because common knowledge and value structures are what underlie aesthetic agreements within a culture—and hence what distinguish its artworks and aesthetics from those of other cultures. Therefore, future advances in computing aesthetics will require a shift in the focus of artificial intelligence—from computing *information in signals* of artworks to computing *explanations of meanings* by audiences.

Acknowledgments We would like to acknowledge the work by Mr. Shunsuke Hananoi from Keio University who kindly translated the survey and collected responses from Japanese participants.

References

1. Addiss S (2012) The art of haiku: its history through poems and paintings by Japanese masters. Shambhala, Boston
2. Addiss S, Yamamoto F, Yamamoto A (2007) Haiku humor: wit and folly in Japanese poems and prints. Weatherhill, Boston
3. Arnheim R (1971) Entropy and art: an essay on order and disorder. University of California Press, Berkeley
4. Baddeley A (1992) Working memory. Science 255:556–569
5. Bayes T (1763) An essay toward solving a problem in the doctrine of chances. Philos Trans 53:370–418
6. Bense M (1965) Aesthetica, einfürung in die neue aesthetik. Agis-Verlag, Baden-Baden
7. Berlyne D (1971) Aesthetics and psychobiology. Appleton Century Crofts, New York
8. Birkhoff G (1933) Aesthetic measure. Harvard University Press, Cambridge
9. Blinderman C (1962) T. H. Huxley's theory of aesthetics: unity in diversity. J Aesthetics Art Criticism 21:49–55
10. Burns K (2006) Atoms of EVE': a Bayesian basis for esthetic analysis of style in sketching. Artif Intell Eng Des Anal Manuf 20:185–199
11. Burns K (2012) EVE's energy in aesthetic experience: a Bayesian basis for haiku humor. J Math Arts 6:77–87
12. Burns K (2015) Entropy and optimality in abstract art: an empirical test of visual aesthetics. J Math Arts 9:77–90
13. Burns K (2015) Computing the creativeness of amusing advertisements: a Bayesian model of Burma-Shave's muse. Artif Intell Eng Des Anal Manuf 29:109–128
14. Burns K, Dubnov S (2006). Memex music and gambling games: EVE's take on lucky number 13. Papers from the AAAI workshop on computational aesthetics, WS-06-04. AAAI Press, Menlo Park, pp 30–36

15. Cover T, Thomas J (1991) Elements of information theory. Wiley, New York
16. Cowan N (2001) The magical number 4 in short-term memory: a reconsideration of mental storage capacity. Behav Brain Sci 24:87–114
17. Dubnov S (2003) Non-Gaussian source-filter and independent components generalizations of spectral flatness measure. In: Proceedings of the international conference on independent components analysis, pp 143–148
18. Dubnov S (2010) Information dynamics and aspects of musical perception. In: Argamon S, Burns K, Dubnov S (eds) The structure of style: algorithmic approaches to understanding manner and meaning. Springer, Berlin, pp 127–157
19. Dubnov S, McAdams S, Reynolds R (2006) Structural and affective aspects of music from statistical audio signal analysis. J Am Soc Inform Sci Technol 57(11):1526–1536
20. Ekárt A, Joó A, Sharma D, Chalakov S (2012) Modeling the underlying principles of human aesthetic preference in evolutionary art. J Math Arts 6:107–124
21. Ellsworth P, Scherer K (2003) Appraisal processes in emotion. In: Davidson R, Scherer K, Goldsmith H (eds) Handbook of affective sciences. Oxford University Press, Oxford, pp 572–595
22. Eysenck H (1941) The empirical determination of an aesthetic formula. Psychol Rev 48:83–92
23. Eysenck H (1942) The experimental study of 'good gestalt'. Psychol Rev 49:344–364
24. Eysenck H (1957) Sense and nonsense in psychology. Penguin, Harmondsworth
25. Fry R (1920) Vision and design. Chatto and Windus, London
26. Higginson W, Harter P (1985) The haiku handbook: how to write, teach, and appreciate haiku. Kodansha, New York
27. Hutcheson F (1729) An inquiry into the original of our ideas of beauty and virtue. J and J Knapton
28. Huxley T (1882) On science and art in relation to education. Collected essays Volume III
29. Kreitler H, Kreitler S (1972) Psychology of the arts. Duke University Press, Durham
30. McGrayne S (2011) The theory that would not die: how Bayes rule cracked the enigma code, hunted down Russian submarines, and emerged triumphant from two centuries of controversy. Yale University Press, New Haven
31. Moles A (1966) Information theory and esthetic perception. University of Illinois Press, Urbana
32. Nake F (2012) Information aesthetics: an heroic experiment. J Math Arts 6:65–75
33. Oatley K (2003) Creative expression and communication of emotions in the visual and narrative arts. In: Davidson R, Scherer K, Goldsmith H (eds) Handbook of affective sciences. Oxford University Press, Oxford, pp 481–502
34. Parsons M (1987) How we understand art: a cognitive developmental account of aesthetic experience. Cambridge University Press, Cambridge
35. Phillips F, Norman J, Beers A (2010) Fechner's aesthetics revisited. Seeing and Perceiving 23:263–271
36. Reichhold J (2002) Writing and enjoying haiku: a hands-on guide. Kodansha, Tokyo
37. Rigau J, Feixas M, Sbert M (2008) Informational aesthetics measures. IEEE Comput Graphics Appl 28:24–34
38. Ross B (2002) How to haiku: a writer's guide to haiku and related forms. Tuttle, Tokyo
39. Rowsome F (1965) The verse by the side of the road: the story of Burma-Shave signs and jingles with all 600 of the roadside rhymes. Plume, New York
40. Scha R, Bod R (1993) Computationele esthetica. Informatie en Informatiebeleid 11(1):54–63. http://iaaa.nl/rs/compestE.html. Accessed 11 June 2014
41. Scherer K (1999) Appraisal theory. In: Dalgleish T, Power M (eds) Handbook of cognition and emotion. Wiley, New York, pp 637–663
42. Shannon C, Weaver W (1949) The mathematical theory of communication. University of Illinois Press, Urbana

43. Silvia P (2005) Emotional responses to art: from collation and arousal to cognition and emotion. Rev Gen Psychol 9:342–357
44. Silvia P (2006) Exploring the psychology of interest. Oxford University Press, New York
45. Stiny G, Gips J (1978) Algorithmic aesthetics: computer models for criticism and design in the arts. University of California Press, Berkeley
46. Yasuda K (1957) The Japanese haiku: its essential nature, history, and possibilities in English. Tuttle, Boston

Chapter 3
Information Sensibility as a Cultural Characteristic: Tuning to Sound Details for Aesthetic Experience

Abstract The question of effectively communicating an artwork in a cultural context relies on joint understanding of certain creative conventions that are shared between an artist and his audience. Modeling of such cultural entrainment requires representation of a style that is specific to each genre, a task that depends in turn on particular compositional rules and aesthetic sensibilities of each culture. In this chapter we extend our previous research on machine learning of musical style into a broader approach of modeling aesthetic communication. The underlying cognitive assumption of our model is that listener's experience of music is a process of actively seeking explanation by reducing the complexity of an incoming stream of sound through a process of approximation and prediction. Musical Information Dynamic is an analysis method that measures changes in the amount of information contents of musical signal over time. Motivated by semiotic analysis, we apply information dynamics analysis in order to measure the tradeoff between accuracy or level of approximation of a signal as captured by its basic units, and its overall information contents derived from its repetition structure. This approach allows us to formally analyze cultural communication in terms of aesthetic and poietic levels in paradigmatic analysis. Comparisons of flute recordings from Western and Far Eastern cultures show that optimal sensibilities to acoustic nuances that maximize the amount of information carried through larger structural elements in music are culture dependent.

3.1 Introduction

Viewing artistic creation as a communication process between an artist and his audience has its roots in semiotic approaches to art analysis where human culture is considered as a collection of signs and the human role in attending to an art artifact is one of making sense of these signs [3]. It is evident that physical properties of the cultural artifact itself, such as colors and sounds of the artistic object, are effectively translated in the viewer's or listener's mind to some abstract data points through a process of perception first and cognition later, where she or he are trying to make

© The Author(s) 2016
S. Dubnov et al., *Cross-Cultural Multimedia Computing*,
SpringerBriefs in Computer Science, DOI 10.1007/978-3-319-42873-4_3

sense of the arriving information. Accordingly, the specific representation of an image or a sound could have very different meanings depending on human ability to perceive their detail and then structure it further into higher level cognitive constructs in a specific cultural and stylistic context.

In this chapter we present a model of aesthetic communication that is based on information theory and machine learning applied to music. Our approach builds upon the human ability to detect patterns and regularities, such as repetitions in a sound as a way to reduce uncertainty about the acoustic signal. Moreover, in the case of music, our model tunes itself to find the most informative representation of a sound that uses the past to predict the future. Application of machine learning have become abundant in music research, mostly in the field of music information retrieval where computers are trained to extract features from sounds for tasks of recognition and retrieval. But listening to music in an aesthetic manner is unlikely to be equated to a process of tagging or labeling of sound events into predefined categories. Not only an aesthetic perception is a more fluid process having ambiguous categories and undetermined relations between sound elements, but also the process of listening itself can not be paralleled to an interpretative action of relating sound to categories outside of the music itself. Even in cases where music serves extra-musical activities such as dance, ceremonial or decorative purposes, the act of listening follows it own inherent musical dynamics that influence the listener through the process of capturing the structure of the music specific to that piece. Listening to music from different cultures often requires different perception of sonic detail by listeners who are trained to pay attention to various levels of musical expression. Constructing mental representations involves memorization and anticipation at different levels of music detail from paying attention to slightest sonic changes in some cases to ignoring some sonic inflections and focusing on more salient aspects of sound structure in other cases.

It had been commonly recognized that differences in appreciation of western versus non western music reside not only in enculturation of their musical systems, such as specifics of their tonal and rhythmic principles, but that these differences also build upon deeper psychophysical dimensions that capture aesthetic, stylistic and emotional conventions of a culture. These differences may be revealed across different forms of art and possibly related to broader aspects of spirituality and philosophy. According to this view, the differences in aesthetics across cultures might be characterized by considering the differences in the ways our brains process information after being exposed to that culture's forms of artistic expression. In other words, we assume that maximizing computational criteria, such as finding the best predictive computer model of a specific musical recording, has parallels in the ways human brains are entrained to capture aesthetic sensibilities that are typical to that piece, or may be genre or even broader culture. We do that by constructing and comparing computer models of musical works from different cultures using a novel approach called "music information dynamics". This approach presents a first step towards a computational model of musical cognition that allows analysis of such sensibilities.

3.1.1 Information Dynamics

Information dynamics analysis assumes that listener's experience of music is a process of actively seeking explanation of music by tracking evolution of its information contents over time. By deriving an optimal representation of music in terms of constructing most informative representation, the method finds the most amount of structure in a recording in terms of maximizing the amount of approximate repetitions it finds in the audio signal. This approach relates questions of perception to the ability of tracing and unfolding of musical information over time. Accordingly we can learn about differences between cultures by considering the differences in musical information processing that derives an optimal representation of the artistic artifacts of the culture in a computationally quantifiable sense.

To understand this approach we first develop a model of human perception that is based on principles of information processing, where both time and complexity are considered together. In this model the ability of the system to minimize surprise or uncertainty over time depends on the number of pattern classes that are detected. In our analysis we go through a process of implicit symbolization where musical elements are identified in contextual manner, depending on relations that are established between these elements over time. This model bears resemblance to the EVE′ model of the second chapter in the sense that it shares the basic premises of a temporal model that assumes that our brain perceives an aesthetic experience through a process of establishing expectations, and subsequent validation or denial of these expectations. While EVE′ is more of a probabilistic Bayesian approach, our Information Rate (IR) model takes an information theoretical view, where aspects of channel and information transmission in conditions of approximate, or so called "lossy" communication serve as our principal tool and concepts for music understanding.

The structure of this chapter is as follows: at the outset we formulate our hypothesis about the relation between aesthetic perception and information seeking behavior. This allows linking formal computational models of information dynamics to those of music cognition, broadly drawing a relation between the role of anticipations and information theoretic tools for characterizing predictive properties of a message.

3.2 Information Seeking as an Aesthetic Perception

It is commonly acknowledged that many animals, and especially humans, seem constantly to seek knowledge and information driven by curiosity—the burning desire to know and understand [15]. Information seeking in general obeys the imperative to reduce uncertainty and can be extrinsically or intrinsically motivated. In extrinsically motivated behavior, information gathering is used to achieve an external objective goal. In intrinsically motivated contexts, on the other hand, the search for information is a goal in itself, a process we would intuitively call curiosity or interest. The fact that animals, and particularly humans, seem avidly to seek out information without an apparent ulterior motive suggests that the brain generates intrinsic rewards that assign value to information, and raises complex questions regarding the benefits and computations of such rewards.

3.2.1   Information Dynamics and Music Cognition

The research on modeling musical cognition involves multiple perception modalities, with expectancies playing one of the central roles in shaping the experience of musical structure. An idea put forward many years ago by music theorists such as Meyer and Narmour states that listening to music consists of forming expectations and continual fulfillment or denial thereof [21, 22]. Information theoretic measures of audio structure have been proposed in attempt to characterize musical contents from an information processing perspective. These methods employ statistical and information theoretic tools to analyze musical predictive structure [1, 10, 11, 27]. These measures consider statistical relations between past, present and future in signals, and include predictive information that measures the mutual information between limited past and the complete future, information rate that measures information between unlimited past and the immediate present and predictive information rate that combines past and future in view of a known present. Additional models of musical expectancy structure build upon short and long term memory neural networks and predictive properties that are local to a single piece versus broader knowledge collected through corpus based analysis. The underlying assumption in investigation of Musical Information Dynamics is that the changes in information content that could be measured in terms of statistical properties such as entropy and mutual information, correlate with musically significant events, which in parallel could be captured by cognitive processes related to music perception and acquired through exposure and learning of regularities present in a corpus of music in a certain style. These models may provide an explanation for the inverted-U relationship often found between simple measures of randomness (e.g. entropy rate) and judgments of aesthetic value [28].

3.2.2   Musical Information: Structure Versus Meaning

Computer modeling of music within a cultural framework requires capturing the idiomatic means of expression that are specific to each such genre. In our research we build computer systems that use machine learning to construct models of music in a specific style. We do this by analysis of musical recordings, relying on the data itself to reveal its structuring principles. This process requires solving musical information modeling problems on two levels: understanding the basic building blocks of music, such as choice of the parameters such as pitch, timbre or harmonic structures used to create a musical fabric, and then capturing sequential aspects of music that tell a musical "story" or create a narrative by structuring basic musical elements over time. In technical terms, we need to solve here the semantic gap problem on two levels: first we need to determine the relation between physical properties of sound or features that can be extracted from the audio signal versus their "meaning" for human listeners, and then also understand how such atoms of musical meaning sequence together into a meaningful message.

Apparently, as we will argue in this chapter, these two stages are inseparable, and their relation is an important characteristic of musical culture. We believe that universally an experience of music relies on establishing, and later denial or fulfillment of musical expectations. Such expectations use past experiences to predict the future, and thus aspects of time and musical structure are intrinsically combined with our ability to find structure over time. But music is a continuous physical phenomenon. It comprises of frequencies that combine into notes and rhythms, but these musical theoretical notions assume a process of categorization or reducing continuous physical measures into discrete categories. As we will see below, the extent to which variations in musical parameters or their corresponding acoustic features can be discretized into categories bears a clear and immediate tradeoff on the overall ability to detect larger structure in the musical composition.

Issues of musical semantics are usually debated between so called referentialist and absolutist points of view. The referentialist view claims that musical meaning comes either from references to objects outside music, while the absolutist view espoused by the composer Igor Stravinsky, argues that the meaning of music, if any, lies in the music itself and the relations entertained by the musical forms. Compromise between these two views was presented as early as 1950 by Meyer who formed a theory of expectations which brings emotion and meaning to music [21]. Meyer used psychologically-based arguments to claim that

> the meaning of music lies in the perception and understanding of the musical relationships set forth in the work of art [thus being primarily intellectual] and that these same relationships, are in some°sense capable of exciting feelings and emotions in the listener.

These ideas were later elaborated by Narmour using the notion of expectation, correlating meaning to the act of establishing musical expectation, only to be later deceived or violated. Without committing to any particular theory, these works seem to suggest the general principle that access to music requires association among musical structures and possibly choosing among a multitude of interpretations and representations of meanings. The central challenge in this research is discovering what aspects of musical structure actually have the evidence of eliciting musical experience.

More recently, music researchers have extended this line of inquiry into a general theory of expectation that involves multiple functionally distinct response systems [8, 31]. Being able to discover musical structure on different time scales and make correct short- and long-term predictions or explanations is essential for music understanding and experience. The anticipatory paradigm of music perception also suggests close relations between the prediction and repetition aspects of music and the aesthetic possibilities afforded by expectation including physiological psychology of awe, laughter, and more [16]. In attempt to provide a formal computational approach to these ideas, an information theoretic construct called information rate (IR) was proposed as a tool to make local maps within an audio recording of the rising and falling rate of musical novelty on different time scales [11, 13]. This necessitates operating not on the raw audio signal but on dimensionally reduced, psychoacoustically aware frame based analyses. The method for measuring information rate was extended towards using the powerful Audio Oracle representation that had been previously used successfully for machine improvisation [14]. This new direction links research on style modeling to research on anticipation, and opens new possibilities for constructing listening agents that are capable of interactive or autonomous improvisation and aesthetic decision making.

3.2.3 Paradigmatic Analysis Revisited

Explaining the meaning of music based on anticipation alone is insufficient. Moreover, considering individual sonic events, such as short frames of sound or representation in terms of their physical or perceptual properties or features can not be considered as signifiers carrying units of meaning on their own. Paradigmatic analysis tries to systematize the process of semiotic analysis by separating the steps of identifying and differentiation among salient elements in a message that are referred to as paradigms, versus the process of analyzing the combinations or "chaining" of such elements into meaningful units called syntagms. In music, paradigmatic analysis was proposed by Ruwet [29] and later extended by Nattiez's [23] who introduced three distinct levels: (a) the neutral level where immanent configurational properties of a musical work are analyzed, (b) the poietic level aimed at capturing compositional procedures and intentions and (c) the aesthetic level of interpretation and perceptual processes. In this respect, the information theoretic analysis proposed here addresses mainly the neutral level through offering tools for discovery of salient musical structures and analysis of their statistics. Although Nattiez claims for independence of the neutral level from the two other aspects by saying that "This is a level of analysis at which one does not decide a priori whether the results generated by a specific analytic proceeding are relevant from the aesthetic or poietic point of view.... 'Neutral' means both that the poietic and aesthetic dimensions of the object have been 'neutralised'", he admits that there is an inherent ambiguity in applying it to music since, "Analysis never stops engineering a dialectical oscillation among the three dimensions of the object. Analysis at the neutral level is dynamic; it displaces itself constantly as the analysis takes place..." [24]. Accordingly, the ability to understand the compositional procedures or perceptual processes depends on the ability to identify the salient musical elements, and vice versa, the criteria set for isolating musical structures might be driven by a desire to achieve maximal poietic (compositional) or aesthetic (perceptual) effect. Motivated by this ambiguity, we shall perform multiple structural analyses of a musical piece through a process of identifying approximate repetitions. Determining the approximation level immediately alters the overall information contents of the resulting analysis, which can formulated in terms of signal complexity or predictability. It should be noted that ideas from information theory have served as an inspiration for computational measure of aesthetics for many years [4, 28]. Such notions consider the aesthetic tradeoff between unity and variety in a message, formalized in terms of differences in signal uncertainly or complexity expressed through measures such as entropy before and after applying a compression algorithm. In temporal signals, such as audio and music, compression often exploits the past of a signal to predict the future, thus reducing the uncertainty about the signal from some initially high variance level to a smaller remaining uncertainty of the prediction error. The notion of Information Rate, which is a measure of Information Dynamics to be introduced below, uses these notions of complexity measured in terms of data size before and after applying an encoding based on the repetitions captured by our analysis. The ability to find approximate repetitions depends on the ability to distinguish or ignore differences among individual sonic events represented in terms of audio features. The search over a space of different models parametrized by a threshold of acoustic similarity can thus be considered as a process of tuning the level structural analysis with an objective to find a representation with highest Information Rate and thus the highest computational aesthetic value. Identification of salient musical structures such as musical motifs is done for a model giving the highest information rate value. We will also argue that the overall profile of Information Rate as function of the acoustic sensibility threshold is an interesting characteristic of musical signals that might be indicative of their cultural differences.

3.3 The Variable Markov Oracle (VMO) Model: Capturing the Past to Predict the Future

In order to predict or explain musical data as it unfolds in time, reference to previous occurrences of similar events are established. The difficulty with finding such past references is twofold: first, the length of memory may vary since the new evidence might have already repeated itself in the past as a continuation of other short or long events. For example, a certain note may tend to repeat itself after another particular note, establishing a repeated short motif of two notes, or this note might be found as part of a longer melody, thus becoming part of a whole sequence of past events. Since many of these different situations may occur in music, how should we establish the correct context, or which memory should we choose to make the best prediction or explanation of new music materials? In this chapter we suggest a motif driven approach where the longest repeated instance of the immediate past (technically called "repeated suffix", since it appears at the end of the current musical sequence) is used as the memory reference in order to explain the present and predict the future.

There are multiple methods that allow capturing relations between past and future in symbolic sequences. It is also important to note that unlike continuous signals that rely on specific time series models, symbolic sequences are often modeled generically through keeping count of appearances of successions of symbols, such as simple count of the relative number of appearances of symbols for zero order Markov model, keeping count of pairs of symbols and conditional counts on appearance of second symbol given a particular symbol one step earlier, which amounts effectively to first order Markov model, and so on. One particular advantage and at the same time difficulty of using symbolic sequences for prediction is the variable order nature of musical memory, or in other words it is unclear how long into the past one should look in order to condition the statistics of a next symbol appearance. We explored various types of string matching methods for prediction in modeling of musical style [9]. Specifically, we compared using of so called Incremental Parsing (IP) based on the Lempel-Ziv compression, and Probabilistic Suffix Trees (PST), as ways of constructing context trees that represented significant factors or subsequences in the original musical symbolic data. In [2] we extended this to the use of Factor Oracle (FO) proposed by M. Crochemore, for the purpose of sequence generation in a particular style [18]. FO automation provides the desired tool for efficiently generating new sequences of symbols based on the repetition structure of the reference example. Compared to IP and PST, the FO model is structurally closer to a generic suffix tree. Its computational efficiency is close to IP (linear, incremental). Moreover, it is an automaton, rather than a tree, which makes it easier to handle maximum suffixes in the generation process. This method also differs from Markov chain based style machines mentioned above in terms of the extent of signal history or past context that it is able to capture.

The use of FO for generation is shown in Fig. 3.1. In order to use the automation for generation, another set of links $S(i) = j$, called Suffix Links running backward

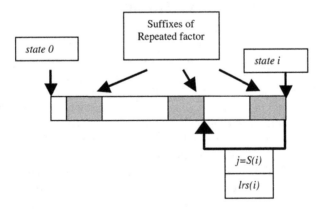

Fig. 3.1 Suffix links and repeated factors i

are used. These links point to node j at the end of the longest repeating suffix (also called repeating factor) appearing before node i (i.e. longest suffix of prefix of i that appears at least twice in prefix of i).

3.3.1 Motif Discovery

Discovering musical patterns (motifs, themes, sections, etc.) requires identifying salient musical elements that repeat at least once within a piece [5, 17]. These patterns could potentially be overlapping with each other and not covering the whole piece in contrast to the "segments" found by music segmentation task [20]. In addition, the occurrences of these patterns could be inexact in terms of harmonization, rhythmic pattern, melodic contours, etc. Discovering patterns in musical pieces of either symbolic or audio representations has been investigated [17] and is of interest to the broad community of both music and signal processing. In this chapter the focus is on pattern discovery from audio recordings. For a comprehensive review on studies of symbolic representations, the readers are referred to [17]. Previous researches on pattern discovery from audio recordings either used F0 estimation (F0 stands for fundamental frequency) with beat tracking techniques to enable geometric representation methods on audio recordings [6] or extended music segmentation techniques with greedy search algorithms [25, 26].

In this research we use *Variable Markov Oracle* (*VMO* hereafter) as the basis of the proposed analytical framework. Our approach differs from other approaches mentioned above in the sense that measures of music information dynamics are used to identify the musical structure for the pattern discovery task. *VMO* was first proposed in [32–34] for devising an efficient audio query matching algorithm. In this work, we additionally exploit the capability of *VMO* to find repeated sub clips in a signal in an unsupervised manner, as described in Wang and Dubnov [33, 34]. As described earlier in this chapter, research in music information dynamics focuses on quantifying the inherent structure of music signals from an information theoretic perspective. Measurements derived from music information dynamics are used in musicological research of notated or symbolic music representation [27], extended to the case of audio recordings in [10]. The over all idea is to use statistical analysis as indicators of significant structural changes, which allow in turn to offer a principled way of applications of music structure analysis and melody phrase identification to musical problems, such as those described in this chapter. *VMO* is a data structure capable of symbolizing a signal by clustering the feature frames in the signal, derived from *Factor Oracle* (*FO* hereafter) [18] and *Audio Oracle* (*AO* hereafter) [12]. *FO* is a variant of suffix tree devised for retrieval of patterns from a symbolic sequence. *AO* is the signal extension of *FO* capable of indexing repeated sub clips of a signal sampled at discrete time, and has been applied to audio query [7], audio structure discovery [14] and machine improvisation [30].

3.3.2 The Oracle Structure

VMO is a suffix tree data structure for multivariate time series devised for query guided audio content generation [32] and multimedia query matching [33, 34]. VMO is capable of finding embedded linkages between samples along the multivariate time series and enables us to devise a Viterbi-like dynamic programming query matching algorithm. In this section we provide the descriptions of the VMO data structure and its model selection criteria.

VMO quantizes a signal O, sampled at time t, into a symbolic sequence $Q = q_1$, q_2, ..., q_t, ..., q_T, with T states and with frame $O[t]$ labeled by a symbol q_t. It does so by constructing a data structure called Factor Oracle (FO). Although the detailed description of the FO structure and construction algorithm is beyond the scope of this paper, we will provide a short overview of the FO structure below. One should note that FO was originally designed for symbolic sequences, and in order to use it with audio signals the signal needs to symbolized into a finite set of labels. We do that by using a distance function with a threshold that determines when two audio features are similar or not. Finally we use an Information Rate (IR) criteria to select the most informative FO among the different FO's created with different thresholds, as will be explained in Sect. 3.3.3.

In order to explain the FO structure, it is sufficient to note that it contains two types of links, forward link and suffix link. Suffix link is a backward pointer that links state t to k with $t > k$, without a label and is denoted by $sfx[t] = k$. Suffix links are used to find the longest repeated suffix in Q. In order to track the longest repeated suffix at each time index t, the length of the longest repeated suffix at each state t is computed by the algorithm described in [18] and is denoted by $lrs[t]$. lrs is essential to the online construction algorithm of an oracle structure and its model selection [14] for *AO* and *VMO*.

Forward links are links with labels and are used to retrieve any of the factors from Q. An oracle structure has two types of forward links; the first is an internal forward link which is a pointer from state $t - 1$ to t labeled by the symbol q_t, denoted as $\delta(t - 1, q_t) = t$. The other forward link is an external forward link which is a pointer from state t to $t + k$ labeled by q_{t+k} with $k > 1$ that share the same label. Forward links provide an efficient way to retrieve any of the factors of Q, starting from the beginning of Q and following the path formed by forward links. We exploited forward link's functionality by treating forward links as indications of possible transitions from state to state for our time series query-by-content tasks.

The last piece needed for the construction of *VMO* is the threshold value, θ. θ is used to determine if the incoming $O[t]$ is similar to one of the frames following the suffix link started at $t - 1$. *VMO* assigns two frames, $O[i]$ and $O[j]$, the same label if $\|O[i] - O[j]\| \le \theta$. In extreme cases, setting θ to very low leads to *VMO* assigning different labels to every frame in O, and setting θ too high leads to *VMO* assigning the same label to every frame in O. As a result, both extreme cases are incapable of

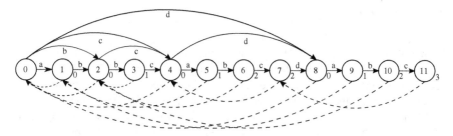

Fig. 3.2 A *VMO* structure with symbolized signal {a, b, b, c, a, b, c, d, a, b, c}, *upper* (normal) *arrows* represent forward links with labels for each frame and lower (*dashed*) are suffix links. Values outside of each circle are the lrs value for each state

capturing any informative structures (repeated suffixes) of the time series. In Sect. 3.3.3, we describe the use of *Information Rate* (*IR* hereafter) to select the optimal θ in the context of music information dynamics. We show an example of the oracle structure with extreme θ values in Fig. 3.3.

The difference between *VMO* and its predecessors, *FO* and *AO*, is that *VMO* explicitly assigns labels by gathering states connected by suffix links, while keeping track of the memory size (length of repeated suffix) that led to each forward transition. This effectively creates a first order hidden Markov model where the states represent collection of "hidden" phrases with similar endings, but with a small but important difference from a regular Markov model, which is that the transitions between the states are dependent on the memory length, thus effectively combining a variable memory property into a computationally efficient and well understood model. The on-line construction algorithms of *VMO* are proposed in [32] and not repeated here. An example of a constructed *VMO*, which is an FO structure for a symbolic sequence "abbcabcdabc", is shown in Fig. 3.2.

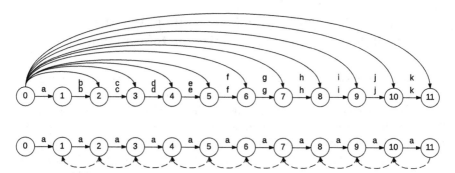

Fig. 3.3 Two oracle structures with extreme values of θ. The characters near each forward links represent the assigned labels. (*Top*) The oracle structure with θ = 0 or extremely low. (*Bottom*) The oracle structure with a very high θ value. It is obvious that in both cases the oracles are not able to capture any structures of the time series

3.3.3 Model Selection

With different θ values, *VMO* constructs different suffix structures and different symbolized sequences from the time series (as shown in Fig. 3.3). To select a sequence with the most informative structures, *IR* is used as the criterion in model selection between the different structures generated by different θ values.

IR measures the relative reduction of uncertainty for a current sample in a time series when past samples are known, averaged over the series. Let the past samples of a time series denoted by $x_{past} = \{x_1, x_2, \ldots, x_{n-1}\}$, the current sample x_n and $H(x) = -\Sigma P(x) \log_2 P(x)$ the entropy of x with $P(x)$ being its distribution. The statistical definition of *IR* is the mutual information between x_{past} and x_n,

$$I(x_{past}, x_n) = H(x_n) - H(x_n | x_{past}) \tag{1}$$

In [14] the above statistical definition of *IR* is replaced by a deterministic notion where $C(\cdot)$ is a compression algorithm or computational measure of time series complexity that replaces the entropy term $H(\cdot)$ in (1).

$$IR(x_{past}, x_n) = C(x_n) - C(x_n | x_{past}) \tag{2}$$

The value of the deterministic *IR* defined in (2) can then be robustly calculated by complexity measures associated with a compression algorithm, where $C(x_n)$ is the number of bits used to compress x_n independently, and $C(x_n | x_{past})$ is the number of bits used to compress x_n using x_{past}. In [19] a lossless compression algorithm, *Compror*, based on *FO* is provided and is demonstrated to have similar performance to *gzip* and *bzip2*. The detailed formulations of how *Compror*, *AO* and *IR* are combined is provided in [14]. We use *Compror* for computing the $C(\cdot)$ function.

3.4 Neutral, Aesthetic and Poietic: Tuning Acoustic Sensibility in Order to Maximize the Information Rate

As explained above, VMO captures the structure of a signal by adapting the threshold at which it is distinguishing between audio features, so as to maximize the overall predictive properties of the FO model, measured in terms of its Information Rate. We shall call this graph "IR Profile" in the discussion to follow. Borrowing from the paradigmatic analysis approach one may view this process as tuning the level of sensibility to changes in acoustic features that effectively determine the basic paradigmatic units so that they give an overall highest result at the aesthetic level. At the following step, the model is used to perform motif extraction, which is commonly considered as a property of the poietic level. Accordingly, the main hypothesis suggested in this charter is that differences in sensibilities to sound variations that can be determined mathematically in terms of the total signal information contents as modeled by VMO, are also playing role in perception of music on the aesthetic level and determine its structure on the poietic level.

3.4.1 Choice of Experimental Repertoire

In order to explore the use of IR paradigmatic method for cross cultural analysis, we performed comparative study of four musical works for the flute, two from Western and two from Far East traditions. The western works considered here are Bach, Partita in A Minor, BWV 1013 and Telemann: Fantasia No. 3 in B minor. The non-western works are Shakuhachi traditional Japanese piece and Nanguan classical Chinese music performed on Xiao flute. The duration of the pieces was between 4–5 min, except for Bach partita that was around 9 min in duration. This particular choice of repertoire is intentionally limited to instruments of similar timbre and monophonic music material, while at the same time still allowing for different levels of expressive inflections that are typical to different cultures. In order to test for differences between different types of flutes, we compared two recordings of Teleman's Fantasia, one performed on a modern flute (traverse metal flute) and the other performed on a recorder (wooden beak flute). The recorder, shakuhachi and xiao flutes are end blown, but unlike the recorder, where the player blows into an internal whistle like duct, the shakuhachi and xiao players blow across the flute, which results in different level of pitch and breath control.

3.4.2 Analysis Method

The recordings were analyzed in terms of their timbral and tonal properties by extracting Mel frequency cepstral coefficients (MFCC) and Chroma features.[1] The mfcc feature capture a broad spectral shape describing the timbre of the instrument, while chroma wraps the frequency analysis into bins corresponding broadly to the western twelve pitches. We preferred the chroma analysis to pitch extraction since it captures energies in all frequency ranges, effectively "wrapping" them into one

---

[1]The analysis package is LabROSA from Columbia University http://labrosa.ee.columbia.edu/.

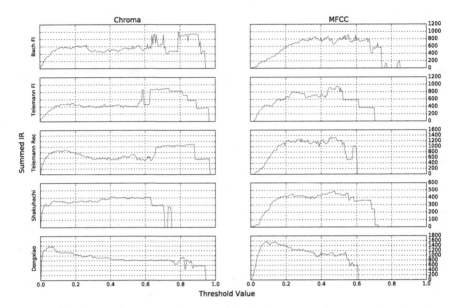

Fig. 3.4 Information Rate Profiles for the Chroma and MFCC features for all five flute pieces. The pieces, from *top* to *bottom*, are: Bach Flute, Telemann Flute, Telemann Recorder, Dongxiao and Shakuhachi. One can note that Western pieces tend to have a large peak at higher thresholds, while far Eastern music examples tend to have higher IR at lower threshold values

octave range, rather than making a hard decision about one fundamental frequency or perceived pitch. This allows chroma also to represent noisy sounds, which would spread the signal energy across multiple chroma bins, while pitch tracking has problems of representing noisy or nonperiodic sounds.

The analysis procedure comprises of the following steps:

- The recording is divided into short sound frames of 23 ms
- Each frame is analyzed in terms of chroma and mfcc features
- The sequence of features were modeled as VMO at different threshold levels for determining when two features are equivalent or different. This results in different VMO structures that capture approximate repetitions at that threshold level.
- Each VMO for mfcc and chroma at a given threshold level was analyzed for its Information Rate (IR) value. This results in an IR Profile for each feature. The results of IR analysis for the five pieces are shown in Fig. 3.4
- A single VMO that corresponds to a threshold value of highest IR was chosen for the motif analysis step. Results of the motifs detected are shown in Fig. 3.5.

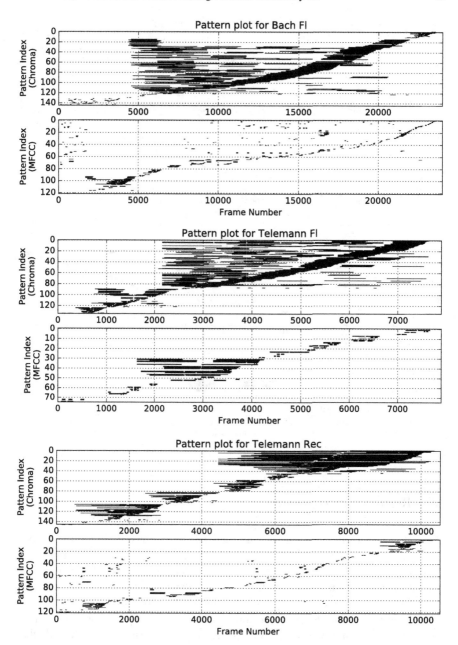

Fig. 3.5 Motifs found in the five Flute pieces using the best VMO for Chroma and MFCC. The *horizontal axis* represents sequence order in time and the vertical axis gives the motif count. Each *horizontal black line* represents an occurrence of a single motif. Shorter motifs correspond to *shorter lines*. The ordering of the motifs is from the end of the piece at the *top*, to the beginning at the *bottom*. This ordering was done for plotting convenience

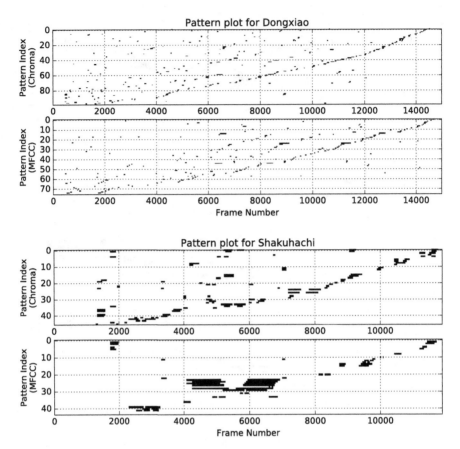

Fig. 3.5 (continued)

3.5   Results and Discussion

The ability to perceive musical structure depends on notions of similarity between acoustical elements that comprise the musical signal. The underlying assumption in construction of a cognitive aesthetic model is that the listener tries to maximize the amount of information he derives from the signal by adapting her or his acoustic sensibilities to make the best overall prediction of the signal. Accordingly, we use IR analysis to find that level of sensibility that gives the most informative representation of the signal. We search for a threshold of similarity using IR profile that accounts for IR values at different thresholds.

In the analysis of IR profiles, shown in Fig. 3.4, we are looking for a point on the IR graph where a value of the threshold found on the x-axis results in the highest IR value shown on the y-axis. These graphs have zero IR value on both threshold extremes since very small threshold values (x-axis near zero) results in practically unpredictable and thus incompressible sequence, while high threshold (x-axis values near 1) reduce the signal to very few basic elements. In such situation the advantage of compression by using the past to more efficiently encode the future is negligible. So in such situation the "uncompressed" complexity and "compressed" complexity are both very small and their difference is zero for high thresholds. One can observe that Western works tend to have larger values at the right side of the curve, i.e. at higher thresholds. Shakuhachi seems to have a wide range of threshold values that have a similar IR level showing as a flat area in the IR profile.

The level of acoustic sensibility is determined in our analysis as the point on the threshold axis that has the highest IR value. This results in a model that captures most of the future of a signal based on its past, where approximate similarity is permissible up to that threshold value. This also results in sequences of signal values that construct motifs, or longer signal segments that are similar on the structural level. The motifs are basic compositional elements of a larger musical piece that according to semiology of music they belong to the "poietic" level. In order to obtain more quantitative estimate of the differences in poietic levels of the different pieces, we extracted repeated sequences, or motifs, from each VMO that was constructed at an optimal threshold level. We further computed statistics of these motifs. The mean and variance of motifs for the different musical works are summarized in Fig. 3.6.

Our results indicate that for Western musical examples our analysis tends to find structure at higher threshold levels, thus favoring coarser sound elements, or in other words Western style is allowing sound units that encompass larger acoustic differences under a single equivalence class. The coarser units result in significantly longer motifs that are apparent for all examples of Western music pieces considered in this experiment. Moreover, in order to test the sensitivity of this analysis to the

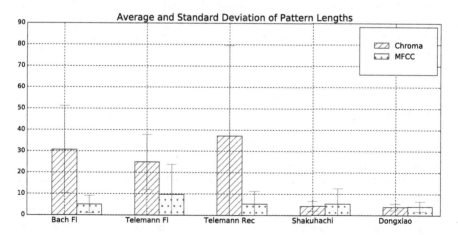

Fig. 3.6 Statistics of the motif lengths for the Chroma and MFCC features found using VMO that was constructed for an optimal threshold at the highest information rate value

physical properties of the instrument we compared analysis of the same musical piece by Telemann performed on a flute and on a recorder. It is interesting to observe that Telemann piece performed on a recorder has a somewhat larger IR peak at lower threshold value. We interpret this finding as an indication that there is an increased amount of structure at the finer sonic detail, which might be indeed related to the nature of the recorder instrument that has a less stable tone and favors more nuances in its sound production.

3.5.1   Multi-level Listening

The method of IR analysis and threshold finding, and it subsequent motif analysis use a single VMO constructed at the optimal threshold value. It is possible that multiple peaks of comparable IR levels would appear for a particular piece. It is also possible that human listening as an explanation seeking behavior exists on multiple levels. In such a case, it is possible that a meaningful musical structure exists at several aesthetic levels at the same time. In such case it is not clear which of the thresholds should be chosen for performing the motif analysis. In other words, since performing syntagmatic analysis (motif finding) depends on the choice of the aesthetic criteria (IR optimal value), difference in aesthetic focus would result in discrepancies in poeitic analysis. Our experience shows that lower thresholds, which correspond to finer acoustic details and thus allowing for smaller sound differences, tend to result in shorter motifs. For instance analysis of Telemann piece performed with the recorder at a value that corresponds to the secondary peak at a lower threshold results in significantly shorter motifs whose statistics are comparable to those found in the Shakuhachi and Dongxiao recordings. Accordingly, our model supports the idea of multiple listening that offers multiple choices for aesthetic expression. The IR profile can be then viewed as an indication of preferences for such levels of listening for a particular piece, possibly also indicative of larger enculturation preferences.

3.6   Disclaimer

It should be clarified that that findings or conclusions regarding the number of motifs or the level of information that is found using the VMO analysis method that searched for maximal peak in the IR profile do not constitute an evaluation or indication of an aesthetic or poietic quality judgment in regards to that piece or culture. We used the terms "aesthetic" and "poietic" in accordance to the common terms used in paradigmatic analysis, without implying any preferences towards particular genre or considering the artistic level of complexity or sophistication of the different genres or cultures.

3.7 Conclusion

In this chapter we presented a computational method to analyze musical structure in terms of detecting approximate repetitions of acoustic features. The level of acoustic detail or sensibilities to nuances in acoustic properties is chosen so as to maximize an information theoretic criteria called Information Rate, a measure that has been previously used for Information Dynamic analysis of musical structure. According to this method, an optimal model was constructed for the level of acoustic sensibility that gives the highest information rate value, which further is used to analyze musical contents in terms of motifs found in that model. The extracted motifs were statistically analyzed for their length in a comparative manner across musical examples of Western and Far Eastern cultures. The findings of this work suggest that different cultures or genres might give preference to different levels of acoustic details, which in turn affects the way larger structural elements, such as motifs, are established. This finding might have important implications for understanding of broader stylistic preferences across genres or cultures, as well as serve as a computational measure for formalization of aesthetic preferences in humans, or as a tool for aesthetic control in computer generated art.

Acknowledgment We would like to thank Mr. Cheng-I Wang from the Center for Research in Entertainment and Learning in UCSD for providing the VMO code and adopting the various VMO algorithms for this research, as well as his help with analysis of the musical examples.

References

1. Abdallah S, Plumbley M (2009) Information dynamics: patterns of expectation and surprise in the perception of music. Connect Sci 21(2-3):89–117
2. Assayag G, Dubnov, S (2004) Using factor oracles for machine improvisation. Soft Comput 8:1–7 (Springer Verlag)
3. Bal M, Bryson N (1991) Semiotics and art history. The Art Bulletin, vol 73, no 2, pp 174–208
4. Bense M (1969) Einfhrung in die informationstheoretische Asthetik. Grundlegung und Anwendung in der Texttheorie (Introduction to the Information-theoretical Aesthetics. Foundation and Application to the Text Theory) Rowohlt Taschenbuch Verlag
5. Collins T (2013) Discovery of repeated themes and sections. http://www.musicir. orgmirexwiki/2013:Discovery_of_Repeated_Themes_Sections. Accessed 4 May 2013
6. Collins T (2014) Sebastian bock, florian krebs, and gerhard widmer, bridging the audio symbolic gap: the discovery of repeated note content directly from polyphonic music audio. In: Audio engineering society conference: 53rd International conference: semantic audio. Audio Engineering Society
7. Cont A, Dubnov S, Assayag G, et al (2007) Guidage: a fast audio query guided assemblage. In: International computer music conference
8. Cont A, Dubnov S, Assayag G (2007) Anticipatory model of musical style imitation using collaborative and competitive reinforcement learning. In: Anticipatory behavior in adaptive learning systems. Springer, Berlin, Heidelberg, pp 285–306
9. Dubnov S, Assayag G, Lartillot O, Bejerano G (2003) Using machine-learning methods for musical style modeling. Comput Mag

10. Dubnov S (2006) Analysis of musical structure in audio and MIDI using information rate. In: Proceedings of international computer music conference (ICMC), New Orleans
11. Dubnov S, McAdams S, Reynolds R (2006) Structural and affective aspects of music from statistical audio signal analysis. J Am Soc Inf Sci Technol 57(11):15261536
12. Dubnov S, Assayag G, Cont A (2007) Audio Oracle: A New Algorithm for Fast Learning of Audio Structures. Proceedings of International Computer Music Conference (ICMC), 2007, Copenhagen, Denmark. ICMA
13. Dubnov S (2008) Unified view of prediction and repetition structure in audio signals with application to interest point detection. IEEE Trans Audio Speech Lang Process 16(2):327–337
14. Dubnov S, Assayag G, Cont A (2011) Audio oracle analysis of musical information rate. In: The fifth IEEE international conference on semantic computing, Palo Alto
15. Gottlieb J, Oudeyer PY, Lopes M, Baranes A (2013) Information seeking, curiosity, and attention: computational and neural mechanisms. Trends Cog Sci 17(11):585–593
16. Huron D (2006) Sweet Anticipation: Music and the Psychology of Expectation. MIT Press, 2006
17. Janssen B, Haas WB, Volk A, Kranenburg P (2013) Discovering repeated patterns in music: potentials, challenges, open questions. In: 10th international symposium on computer music multidisciplinary research. Laboratoire de Mecanique et d Acoustique
18. Lefebvre A., Lecroq T, Compror (2002), On-line lossless data compression with a factor oracle, Information Processing Letters 83 (2002) 1–6
19. Lefebvre A, Lecroq T, Alexandre J (2003) An improved algorithm for finding longest repeats with a modified factor oracle. J Automata Lang Combin 8(4):647–657
20. McFee B, Ellis DPW (2014) Analyzing song structure with spectral clustering. In: The 15th international society for music information retrieval conference, pp 405–410
21. Meyer LB (1956) Emotion and meaning in music. Chicago University Press, Chicago
22. Narmour E (1990) The analysis and cognition of basic melodic structures: the implication-realization model. University of Chicago Press
23. Nattiez J-J (1975) Fondements d'une Smiologie de la Musique. Union Gn-rale d'Editions, Paris
24. Nattiez J-J (1990) Music and discourse: towards a semiology of music. Princeton University Press, Princeton
25. Nieto O, Farbood M (2013) MIREX 2013: Discovering musical patterns using audio structural segmentation techniques. Music Information Retrieval Evaluation eXchange, Curitiba, Brazil
26. Nieto O, Farbood M (2014) Identifying polyphonic patterns from audio recordings using music segmentation techniques, In: The 15th international society for music information retrieval conference
27. Potter K, Wiggins GA, Pearce MT (2007) Towards greater objectivity in music theory: Information-dynamic analysis of minimalist music. Musicae Scientiae 11(2):295–322
28. Rigau J, Feixas M, Sbert M (2008) Informational aesthetics measures. IEEE Comput Graph Appl
29. Ruwet N (1972) Language, musique, posie. Editions du Seuil, Paris
30. Surges G, Dubnov S (2013) Feature selection and composition using pyoracle. In: The 9th artificial intelligence and interactive digital entertainment conference
31. Tillmann B, Kronland-Martinet R, Ystad S, Jensen K (eds) (2008) Music cognition: learning, perception, expectations: CMMR 2007, LNCS 4969, p 1133
32. Wang C, Dubnov S (2014) Guided music synthesis with variable markov oracle. In: The 3rd international workshop on musical metacreation, 10th Artificial intelligence and interactive digital entertainment conference
33. Wang C, Dubnov S (2015) Pattern discovery from audio recordings by variable markov oracle: a music information dynamics approach In: Proceedings of 40th IEEE internatinoal conference on acoustics, speech and signal processing, Brisbane
34. Wang C, Dubnov S (2015) The variable markov oracle: algorithms for human gesture applications. Multi Media IEEE 22(4):52–67

Printed in the United States
By Bookmasters